Ashes

ASHES

a play by

DAVID RUDKIN

Talonbooks · Vancouver · Los Angeles · 1978

Talonbooks   Talonbooks
201 1019 East Cordova   P.O. Box 42720
Vancouver   Los Angeles
British Columbia V6A 1M8   California 90042
Canada   U.S.A.

This book was typeset by Linda Gilbert of B.C. Monthly
Typesetting Service, designed by David Robinson and
printed by John Deyell Company for Talonbooks.

First printing: October 1978

Talonplays are edited by Peter Hay.

Canadian Cataloguing in Publication Data

   Rudkin, David, 1936—
   Ashes

   ISBN 0-88922-135-9

   I. Title.
   PR6068.U34A8 1978   822'.9'14   C78-002185-1

to Sandra

Ashes was first performed at the Open Space Theatre in London, England, on January 9, 1974, with the following cast:

Colin	Peter McEnery
Anne	Lynn Farleigh
Doctor, Surgeon, Guru	Ian Collier
Jennifer, Receptionist, Valerie	Penny Ryder

Directed by Pam Brighton
Designed by William Dudley

Ashes was also performed at the Young Vic Theatre in London, England, on June 9, 1976, with the following cast:

Colin	Ian McKellen
Anne	Gemma Jones
Doctor, Surgeon, Guru	Paul Shelley
Jennifer, Rectptionist, Valerie	Ann Mitchell

Directed by Ron Daniels
Designed by Andrea Montag

Ashes had its American premiere at the Mark Taper Forum in Los Angeles, California, on April 3, 1976, with the following cast:

Colin	Michael Cristofer
Anne	Tyne Daly
Man	James Ray
Woman	Andra Akers

Directed by Edward Parone
Designed by Sally Jacobs

Ashes was also performed at the Manhattan Theatre Club in New York City, New York, on December 8, 1976, with the following cast:

Colin	Brian Murray
Anne	Roberta Maxwell
Man	John Tillinger
Woman	Penelope Allen

Directed by Lynn Meadow
Designed by John Lee Beatty

This production was transferred by the New York Shakespeare Festival to the Anspacher Theatre on February 8, 1977.

LIST OF CHARACTERS

COLIN, in his early thirties, *Northern Irish, was a writer, now a teacher.*
ANNE, in her late twenties, *his wife, West Riding, was an actress, now a teacher.*

An averagely presentable couple, neither sexually glamourous nor pathetically unprepossessing. COLIN cared more how he dressed five years ago — a good pair of unflared corduroys he wore for best then, he uses at work today; plain shirt, tie, quilted anorak, hush puppies. ANNE had more style, but now they live far from shops and have less money — a neutral grey smock, fashionable once, now she knocks about in.

OTHER CHARACTERS

DOCTOR.
JENNIFER, *a medical student.*
SEMINOLOGIST, *the "Guru."*
RECEPTIONIST *at the Guru's.*
GYNAECOLOGICAL SURGEON.
VALERIE, *a fecund neighbour.*
AMBULANCE DRIVER.
NURSE.
SOCIAL SERVICES OFFICER.
AREA ADOPTIONS OFFICER, *Mrs. Jones.*

These roles should be taken by one male and one female actor; but in this doubling there is no thematic significance. To cast each separately is possible, but would tell, I think, against the "minimal" method of the play.

SET

*A small auditorium is preferable. No set as such is called for
— a manoeuvrable rostrum (for bed, couch, etc.); plain
upright chairs; a doctor's desk (perhaps, for variety, two —
one left; one right).*

*On a very small stage, white screens or traverse curtains can
be used to mask, discover, suggest change or location, etc.
On a larger stage, these effects should be sought with light.*

*The clinical processes shown should be at root authentic, but
reduced to a spare theatrical severity. As to the indignities
to which COLIN and ANNE submit themselves, they must
not make light of them, nor ever cheaply clown them; rather,
bring us into a wry factual sharing of them. They may, of
course, tempt us here and there into a tasteless or ignorant
laugh, whereat, with the line that follows, or by their
stillness, deliver any necessary rebuke.*

*The play's running time has ranged from one hundred
minutes to two and a quarter hours. This is not a question
so much of whether a production is a fast or a slow one; it
depends also, of course, on how much, if at all, the audience
laugh during the opening scenes, where most of the humour
is concentrated; but another factor, to which the play is
uniquely susceptible, is the size of the auditorium. If the
actors have to project the text, in order to bring the audience
into something which is essentially intimate, they have to do
so with especial subtlety, and this, in performance, can take
time. In any case, for the sake of the play's three movement
form, it should be played without interval. In the Young Vic
production, a break was made after COLIN's "extinction"
speech on page 65; in Los Angeles, after ANNE's "Mozart,
Darwin" speech on page 64. I do not endorse either procedure.*

one

There is darkness. From speakers around the auditorium, a man's deep rhythmic breathing subsides towards silence. Suddenly, from behind a screen or from slow stage gloom, the thrash and sense of a brief bedtussle is heard.

COLIN: *unseen, with a yelp of trivial pain, voice barely recognizable as Northern Irish, with characteristic "ou" and "r" sounds, and a hint of Antrim tune*
Ow no — do you have to do that now?

ANNE: *unseen as well, voice quiet, just recognizable as West Riding, with a trace of a back "a" sound*
When else do I get? Never still enough.

COLIN:
Gouging.

ANNE:
Not gouging.

COLIN:
Each twinge runs to the knackers like some Turkish torture.

ANNE: *mocking*
Poor knackers. . . .

COLIN:
Leave over!

ANNE:
I've nearly got it. . . .

COLIN: *threatening*
I'll pull him out —

ANNE:
There. A lovely huge one, juicy and black. What was so bad about that?

COLIN:
How do you tell in the dark what colour?

ANNE:
I've had me eye on that since before we put the lights out.

COLIN:
Preying mantis'll never be extinct while you're alive.

ANNE:
The human skin must breathe.

COLIN:
You've not been aroused by me at all —

ANNE:
Don't be fatuous —

COLIN:
>All my foreplay reefed on your single expectation of winkling out one clotted pore.

ANNE:
>I like my man to be healthy.

COLIN:
>Post-coital triumph more like. Penis jealousy.

ANNE:
>What? Flatter yourself.

COLIN: *pausing*
>I never had blackheads till you started purging them.

ANNE:
>Not true.

>*She pauses.*

>None of your other bedmates bothered, you mean. Whatever sex they were.

COLIN:
>*They* weren't cannibals.

ANNE: *pausing*
>Getting heavy, love.

COLIN: *put out*
>Sorry.

ANNE: *pausing, quieter now*
>Mop up now.

COLIN:
>Ay. Load delivered, back to yard.

If the audience laughs, cut the following line.

COLIN:
Cold half of bed.

They have separated. There is a long pause.

ANNE:
Perhaps we did it this time.

The lights snap on. COLIN remains on stage, but is not present during the following scene. ANNE's half of the bed is now a doctor's couch on which ANNE lies supine, head towards the audience, bare legs raised in a coital position. The DOCTOR is fresh-faced, in his early thirties, with a slight hint of a farmer about him. Gently, firmly, he palps ANNE's belly to feel that everything is in its proper place.

DOCTOR: *with the faintest trace of rural speech, frank, unpatronizing* How long have you and your husband been trying for a conception, Mrs. Harding?

ANNE:
Two years.

DOCTOR:
Then you *do* have a problem. Forgive me: you are doing it right?

ANNE:
Do we look fools?

DOCTOR:
I've had couples trying to conceive through the navel.

He manipulates, palps.

No sign of damage or deformity, no displacement. . . .

14

Very nice set of organs, Mrs. Harding; compact. . . .
Your husband is potent, you say; your blood groups
compatible; your cycle short and regular —

ANNE: *bitterly*
Clockwork.

DOCTOR:
Which I like. Well. First I think we should take a PC
sample —

ANNE:
Post-coital —

DOCTOR: *surprised that she knows*
Have you been a nurse?

ANNE:
No.

> *The DOCTOR pauses, comes away from her and
> peels off a disposable glove which he throws into
> a wastebasket.*

DOCTOR:
Well you can probably work out for yourself what a
post-coital test involves. Round about the tenth or
eleventh day of your next cycle —

> *Blackout.*

> *In the darkness, the sound of an alarmclock is
> heard. From COLIN and ANNE, the sounds of
> waking and shifting are heard. The alarmclock
> stops.*

ANNE: *yawning, unseen*
God, what an hour? Why so early?

COLIN: *yawning, also unseen*
Specimen, love.

ANNE:
> Mm?

COLIN:
> Specimen. We have to provide a characteristic sample
> of our mixture. Fresh.

ANNE: *miserable, tired*
> Oh fuck —

COLIN:
> Something like that.

ANNE:
> I'll have to take a pee.

> *ANNE is heard stumbling off.*

> Put 'fire on, love.

COLIN: *grumbling, moving*
> Mouth like a bloody parrotcage. . . .

> > *The lights come up slowly — the dim glow
> > of an electric heater. The form of COLIN
> > crouching before the heater is seen. The sound
> > of urine trickling into water is heard; the rip
> > and scuff of toilet paper; the sound of a toilet
> > flushing.*

> Romantic.

> *ANNE returns to bed — a dim shape.*

ANNE: *shuddering*
> Right then. Man. I'm all cold and pissy for you: come
> and give.

> > *She lies head towards the audience, legs raised,
> > opened.*

*The lights come on. JENNIFER, a medical
student wearing a white coat, helps the
DOCTOR throughout the following scene. The
DOCTOR stands bowed at the foot of ANNE's
bed, with some unseen medical implement
which he has inserted between her raised legs.
A careful snipping sound is heard. The DOCTOR
draws the implement out. JENNIFER helps
the DOCTOR transfers a smear to a slide. The
DOCTOR peels off his disposable glove and
throws it into the wastebasket. JENNIFER
takes the slide across the stage to the DOCTOR's
desk and sets it up in a microscope. The
DOCTOR comes over to her and peers into the
microscope. ANNE meanwhile relaxes, sitting
on the bedside. She watches with anxiety.
The DOCTOR finally speaks.*

DOCTOR: *very quietly*
Jennifer.

JENNIFER:
Doctor?

DOCTOR: *still quiet*
These sperms are all dead, wouldn't you say?

JENNIFER: *looking into the microscope*
Oh no, Doctor, I think there's one.

DOCTOR:
One what?

JENNIFER:
One sperm alive.

DOCTOR:
Where?

He looks into the microscope.

17

DOCTOR: *repeating himself*
Where?

JENNIFER:
Five o'clock.

DOCTOR: *seeming at last to find it*
Oh yes. Oh no. Oh no, Jennifer, that's a blemish in the slide.

> *He is quieter now.*

Appointment to see the husband, I think.

> *The lights change. COLIN emerges into view. He is on his side of the bed. His trousers and briefs are down. The DOCTOR disposes of the slide he has been examining, puts on another disposable glove and comes across to COLIN. COLIN stands to have his genitals examined. The DOCTOR partly screens him, professionally observing the patient's privacy.*

COLIN:
The self-consciousness of the situation has shrunk him rather.

DOCTOR: *drolly*
Testicles, not the penis, deliver the goods.

> *He checks to see that COLIN's testicles are free.*

Cough please.

> *COLIN coughs.*

Again.

> *COLIN coughs again.*

No injury at any time?

COLIN:
None.

DOCTOR:
No growth, clotting? . . .

COLIN:
That I know of. . . .

DOCTOR:
No reason why normal testicles should not produce
good semen. Yet you know by the time yours gets
where it matters your semen is useless. I shall give
you a letter —

> *The lights change. The DOCTOR exits. COLIN
> emerges from the appointment pulling up his
> briefs and trousers. He keeps the audience at
> some distance, putting on an act for them.*

COLIN: *imitating a woman receptionist*
"Yes, sir, can I help you?"

> *As his self.*

I have this letter. It is about a sperm count.

> *As the woman.*

"Oh, this is Family Planning. You want Fertility.
Up the stairs, sir."

> *His trousers are up now. He looks at the
> audience, making them feel a little easier with
> his company. He then goes into another act,
> a vocal send-up of a Brummy lab assistant.*

"Here y'are then, friend: a room apart. Produce your
sample, bring it back to the lab when yow've done.

We send yow the bill for two smacker, yowr doctor the result in twenty-one days. Venetian blind don't work, I'm sorry to say, but nobody to overlook yow. Lock on the door don't work either, I'm sorry to say, but they all know here what this room is for."

Speaking confidentially.

"Some blokes has to get their wives to help them wi' this at home, then bring the product in to us by buz. Take your time."

> *COLIN stares out at the audience His expression never breaks, yet somehow he charms the audience into a humorous sharing of his absurd predicament. But nothing must rupture his essential privateness. The sound of shouts and whistling are heard — building site sounds. COLIN glances up once or twice towards these sounds. He takes out of his pocket a tiny glass or plastic container — two inches deep at the most, neck barely an inch across, with a blank label. He looks up at the audience from this container. The building site sounds worry him. Also, there is an additional problem. How is he to address an erection to this container? With simple, precise gestures, he mimes one or two ways that occur to him. They are impossible. He mimes a third way. It is even more absurd. He catches the audience's eye, goes and sits on a chair nearby and stalls for time. A thought occurs to him. He takes out a pencil stub and writes on the label. He stands up and shows the audience what he has written.*

My name. Against confusion.

> *He sits down and drums his fingers. Another thought occurs to him. He puts the container on the floor and all but gets down on all fours above it. He hears a builder's voice calling*

someone. He jumps up sharply and sits down,
container in hand.

Clinic sounds are heard — trolleys in corridors,
someone on an intercom calling for a doctor.
After a moment, COLIN sees that he must make
a real effort. He brings his chair downstage,
drops his trousers and turns his back to the
audience.

Speaking over his shoulder, he says . . .

What are yous expectin' to see, then?

He sits down and makes discreet gestures of
fondling himself. Soon, perhaps, he makes a
little tsk-tsk sound, as though geeing-up a
diminutive horse between his thighs.

Speaking once again, gently, he says . . .

There's a fella. There's a fella.

The sound of a door opening is heard — and the
shriek of a young girl. COLIN jumps up sharply,
covering himself with his hands. The sound of
clattering heels fleeing is heard, then, a stifled
giggle, and more giggles, shared afar.

Speaking over his shoulder, he says . . .

Was ever fella so abused?

The building site sounds are heard again — jolly
whistling, etc. COLIN has an idea.

Speaking to his penis, he says . . .

We'll go an' shufty at the builder boys. There's maybe
a nice arse'll turn ye on.

*Partly hauling his trousers up, he moves off,
hurrying back for the container which he has
forgotten. Finally, he exits. The sounds stop.*

*The lights change. From where COLIN has
exited, the DOCTOR enters. He has a labelled
container in his hand with its milky specimen.
He goes and sits behind his desk.*

DOCTOR:

Colin Harding, his seed. There's life in this, the clinic
tell me: though not so much as I should like.

*COLIN enters, fully dressed. He brings a chair
downstage, in front of the DOCTOR's desk, and
sits on it.*

You could conceive with this semen, Mr. Harding;
but it would be a miracle.

COLIN: *with no aggression, merely accepting*
You mean my seed is sterile?

DOCTOR:

No. A hundred or so million sperms per millilitre a
man ejaculates when making love: only one of these
need reach the ovum to conceive. But all x hundred
million need to be very lively for there to be that
chance.

COLIN:

Mine are not — lively.

DOCTOR:

Too few of them are. They litter this fluid like so
many stunned tadpoles, I'm afraid.

COLIN: *pausing*
Can anything be done.

There is almost no question to his tone.

DOCTOR:

You can help. Use a shower from now, not a bath.
Scrap your tight briefs for boxer shorts. It takes six
weeks to make a sperm, and requires a temperature
in the scrotum two degrees lower than that of the
body. Which is why in hot weather, you will have
noticed, your ballocks dangle. Circulation. So, every
morning and every evening for the next six weeks,
bathe your testicles in the coldest water, several
minutes at a time. At the end of January, go back
for another sperm count. Central heating, you know,
probably reduces male fertility more than any other
factor in the West. I think also you should eat less:
hunger helps fecundity.

*The DOCTOR discreetly disposes of COLIN's
semen specimen into the wastebasket. The
moment should not be lost on the audience.*

*The lights change. COLIN comes forward and
addresses the audience.*

COLIN:

Hands up who's tried bathing his balls? Dangle them
in a bowl, do I hear ye say? Some anatomy: you try
that.

*He mimes sufficient enough to illustrate the
point.*

A flannel, then? Not very effective. Stand akimbo in
the bath, a cold shower aimed upwards?

He mimes this — and mimes getting soaked.

One foot outside the bath then, the other across?

He mimes this, using the chair as the bath.

Marginally improved for access: if you don't mind
cleaning the floor down twice a day. I doubt even a

bidet's not much help in my precise predicament. But for those of you, for those of you who may at some time need it, a solution does emerge. Sit back on the bog pan, your legs priapically wide; grip the showerhead in one hand, in the other exposing the scrotum to its full freezing blast. December. Friends in the house over Christmas —

In a Birmingham speech pattern.

"Mom, what's that funny splashing in the bathroom?" The things a silly sod'll do for fatherhood. Or is it fatherhood? Might it not rather be, for the myth of "manliness?"

He stands up and turns.

Hello, I'm back again.

Answering himself, as if he were the Brummy lab assistant.

"Six weeks on the cold water then, have you, friend? Mind you, can work a charm. In you get then: wanker's paradise. Not my idea of one though. Still: they find it easier the second time."

As himself, drily.

Ay. I thought to pick up this time a certain class of picture book.

As the lab assistant.

"Visual aid?"

As himself.

An honest usage, Longford missed.

He moves off, factually letting the audience
glimpse two skin magazines he has: one of
women and one of young men.

ANNE comes downstage. She is carrying some
letters.

ANNE:

Enter wife, reading aloud for audience's benefit several
convenient letters. Marj is expecting. Valerie is
expecting. Cynthia's in pod again. None of them
planned for. Wendy miscounts on the pill; Hilary's
Albert comes home from a police course randy as
hell, no time for precautions, wham, bam, thank
you, ma'am, hey, ho, another bottle shot from the
shelf. Click from a man's pants, some women.

She reads the last letter.

From the doctor. Sperm motility now normal. Quote,
"If you go overdue, inform me." After three or four
months, I do. First time in my bleeding life, overdue.
I say, "No, it's a freak." Or hysterical. Twenty-nine
days, for me, unheard of. Thirty. He's telling himself,
"Stop thinking about it, stop hoping: watched pot
and that." We've clicked or we haven't. Thirty-one
days. If we can hang on till only Monday, hang out
the flags, I'm qualifying for a urine test! Thirty-two
days. Every time I'm out of the room now, I can hear
his ears pricked for the sound of the door of the
cupboard where I keep my pads. Thirty-third day.
No gutrot. No pain in the back, no heaviness in the
breasts. Just the blood.

She pauses and sits down.

COLIN enters quietly and comes down to her.

COLIN:

Bad one?

He doesn't need telling. He reaches out and touches her, but there is nothing in his touch. In his tenderness, there is something hard, hurt. ANNE turns her head from him, moves her hand across herself, away from him. She sits frozen, not present.

The SEMINOLOGIST enters. He is greying, has short hair, fine-rimmed spectacles and an Edinburgh accent of the professional class.

SEMINOLOGIST: *speaking to the audience*
I am an expensive seminologist. My two new patients dub me the Guru because they get the impression I think I am omniscient. Indeed, I do occasionally speak as though I personally had invented the first idea of everything, including coitus itself.

He sits behind his desk.

The SEMINOLOGIST's RECEPTIONIST comes over to COLIN. She is impeccably manicured, the type of woman that would make a man feel as if he reeked of sweat.

RECEPTIONIST:
Mr. Harding?

COLIN: *following her*
Colin Harding, yes, I have an appointment — Dr. Mc. . . .

RECEPTIONIST:
I'm sure your accent will make Dr. McAnespie feel quite at home. What part of Scotland are you from?

COLIN:
County Antrim.

RECEPTIONIST: *pausing*
Not a very happy place, these days.

COLIN can say nothing to this. The
RECEPTIONIST leaves him sitting opposite
the SEMINOLOGIST. ANNE remains on stage,
but is not present. The SEMINOLOGIST has a
file of letters on his desk in front of him.

COLIN:

Doctor, I am not a superstitious man. Forgive me if
this question sounds benighted. My first erotic urges
— the earliest I remember — were to bite lumps out
of classmates' buttocks in the showers: especially
the hairier ones as I myself was never very hairily
endowed. I'm still tormented with a ravening
homosexual self.

SEMINOLOGIST: *gently*

Oh, there is no such thing as a "homosexual self."
Sexuality runs deeper than culture, how can it
discriminate; why should it, as culture does? You
have a sexual self. That is your central essential
energy, deeper, truer than any cultural self: "homo"
and "hetero" are straws on the surface. A single-sex
school you were at?

COLIN:

Oh, a day one, but very ancient . . . the usual seedbed
of gentle Christian fascism. The cult of the Chap, the
heroic unattainable ideal . . . from which regime an
inadequate like me is expected at nineteen miraculously
to blossom straight. Ten years of my adult emotional
life that schooling cost me, ten maimed years: I know
where I would put a bomb if a Fenian ever gave me
one. No child of mine must ever go to such a place.
I fought hard — not to convert my sexuality from one
orientation to another, but to broaden it to include
the opposite sex as well. I refused to be the stunted
end of a tree. A hard fight; I have won. My sexual
world is very discordant now, but for all the vain
yearning my several lusts put me in, I am glad in their
diversity and would not be without one of them. Out
from this all, my wife is the best thing has happened

me. Now we want children. For years we have had
no luck, and it is explicable — you have the history of
it there. So I ask this. It will sound naive, but this is
now something of a mortal strait for me, and when
our back is to the wall we think irrational things:
Can there be, can there be at all any connection,
any causality, between the homoerotics I still also so
strongly feel and the dying of my seed.

SEMINOLOGIST:
If you believe in a crabbèd heterosexual father God,
you could call your plight a judgement. If you believe
what you are paying me seven old guineas for, then I,
as a man of reason and acquainted with chemistry,
say, "No cause, no cause." Just stretch the skin
tighter over your testicles when you bathe them;
and two minutes only, twice in the day. Continue
the cold water, until you have conceived.

COLIN:
But could worry or stress of any kind? . . . Or if
my work were not going well, or I were at some
professional crisis? . . .

> *The SEMINOLOGIST checks through some*
> *letters in front of him to see what COLIN's*
> *profession is.*

Could anything emotional or psychological? . . .

SEMINOLOGIST: *slightly impatient*
Mr. Harding, you do perform the sexual act?

COLIN:
Yes.

SEMINOLOGIST:
And you ejaculate?

COLIN:
Yes.

SEMINOLOGIST:
> Well. Man's piddling little psyche might hinder
> performance, but not affect one whit the chemical
> quality of what he secretes. The trouble in your
> case most possibly lies with neither wife nor you, but
> in the combination of your two genetic chemistries.

> *He stands up.*

> You are familiar with the routine for the post-coital
> test?

COLIN:
> We have done several.

> *He stands up.*

SEMINOLOGIST: *looking at a letter*
> Here also your diligence has been excessive: there is
> no need for the alarm clock, intercourse the night
> before is quite sufficient.

> *The RECEPTIONIST re-enters. ANNE is present
> once again. The SEMINOLOGIST brings COLIN
> up behind ANNE.*

> Semen is petrol, the engine is the womb: the one
> must merely be brought, effective, to the other.
> I recommend you now, during the fertile period
> of Mrs. Harding's month, to adopt for intercourse
> what I call a posture of performing dogs —

> *The RECEPTIONIST charmingly invites ANNE
> to pose as the SEMINOLOGIST suggests.*

> Your wife on her knees, head down, her buttocks
> spread —

ANNE: *speaking to the audience*
> Dignity.

The RECEPTIONIST bows ANNE's head.
The SEMINOLOGIST brings COLIN up behind
her.

SEMINOLOGIST:
You entering from behind. Which may, in your case, revive certain unorthodox memories. Nevertheless —

He motions to COLIN to kneel closer behind
ANNE, almost to mount her. The RECEP-
TIONIST meanwhile brings out a larger than
life anatomy class cross-section of a phallus and
a similar model of the female genitalia.

You will see how, in this posture, the female tackle flops, affording the penis —

The RECEPTIONIST inserts the phallus. There
is a clicking of parts.

— the most efficient angle of insemination. Compared with which, the conventional Anglo-American attitude —

The RECEPTIONIST withdraws the phallus.
The SEMINOLOGIST rights the model. The
RECEPTIONIST inserts the phallus once again.
There is a clicking of parts.

— from the spermatozoön's point of view, is all uphill.

COLIN and ANNE remain in the posture in
which the SEMINOLOGIST has placed them.
They are clinical objects.

It's all yours.

COLIN:
You'll send us the bill?

RECEPTIONIST:
Of course.

*The RECEPTIONIST and the SEMINOLOGIST
exit. COLIN starts in. The SEMINOLOGIST
re-enters.*

SEMINOLOGIST:
> Mr. Harding, one other thing. We may of course be
> wrong in assuming your sperm count adequate —

> *COLIN stops, interrupted.*

> I'm not altogether satisfied with the procedure at
> that clinic —

> *The RECEPTIONIST re-enters, following the
> SEMINOLOGIST. She brings COLIN a specimen
> container of contrasting, but equally impractical
> design as the one he has been given before.*

> Would you, therefore, as early as you feel able,
> observing the necessary three days' continence
> beforehand, be good enough to furnish a sample at
> your home, returning it well sealed to me by post,
> first class? I can then do a count myself before I
> come to the PC test to see what, if anything, ill-
> befalls your semen in your wife.

> *The SEMINOLOGIST exits, with the
> RECEPTIONIST following him. COLIN moves
> away from ANNE and holds the container,
> addressing the audience.*

COLIN:
> Up again, down again: Jack found fecund, now his
> fecundity in question, now branded barren.

> *Speaking in a tone of mocking self laceration.*

> So, if Jack's lust does after all lack living spore, this
> seems to Jack wondrous like Nature does not select
> him for the Club of Man — the sort, I mean, Nature
> prefers not to continue his kind. I learned to live

with *that* emotion a long time since. Yet: might not
Nature's very discardment of Jack rank Jack a little
higher than the genital beast in Man? *More* man than
Reproductive Man? Paradox. Think. Jack's seed,
qua sterile, is fit for transcendental sport alone;
made, not for breeding, but delight alone; to be shot
singing out, anarchic, athletic, milk in itself, free up
vagina and glad up lad-arse, knob leaving cunt for
joy alone, splitting sphincter and reaming rectum
for joy alone, his bags drained dry through holes in
walls by unseen men's mouths: the naked jissom,
dis-Communion-ized, for play alone.

> *He is quieter now.*

Perhaps there is some sort of evolution here: man's
sex emanicipated from the shackle and the mire of
Propagation; a sexuality dis-familied, detribalized,
fraternal: in this sterility, the seed of that?

> *COLIN goes over to the bed and kneels behind
> ANNE upon it. Wearily, they posture themselves.*

ANNE:
> He functions to order every time. Only once, for
> Guru's PC, he couldn't stay hard, it wouldn't
> penetrate — Surprised? You try it to order on two
> or three fixed nights in the cycle: knowing "Tonight
> or never; the love blend must be there for the doctor
> tomorrow; or for hope of conception this month.
> Or for the doctor anyway." In this posture. He
> probably has to pretend I'm some sailor from his
> misspent youth.

COLIN: *beginning to mount her*
> The acts don't resemble, lovey. Though it is possible
> to fantasize; which, frankly, at times has helped me.

> *Suddenly, he sighs, falls away, lies wretched.*

ANNE:
>Anyway, this one time, for the Guru's PC, he just couldn't stay hard enough to enter. Every effort of mine just made him floppier.

>>*Slowly, she rests on her legs and with her tenderness and her voice, she creates a deeply erotic mood which relaxes him.*

>But in the night, in his sleep, he was starting me. I woke up so turned on. After a while, I went down on him — it was the first time I had ever been moved to do that. He'd come up very heavy and strong; the knob felt so burgeoning and gorgeous. So, half-asleep, we managed it after all. So we've never, in all these years — for doctor or calendar — never once failed to deliver. On occasions like the one I describe, he can be quite a satyr. Appearances deceive.

COLIN:
>It's better at such times, love, the better you help me.

ANNE: *not breaking the mood till the very end*
>I thought after that one, I thought if the quality of the act itself has anything to do with it and we haven't clicked this time, then there's no fucking justice in the thing.

>>*Bitterly, she turns away. COLIN remains there, but is not present.*

>>*The SEMINOLOGIST enters briskly. Quietly, he comes over to ANNE and gently, he postures her, turning her over on her left side, her right leg crooked up. She speaks to the audience.*

>This man is a *specialist*. He examines in the Sims position. Not like your National Health.

>>*She lies back down ready for her examination. The SEMINOLOGIST makes the minimal*

> *sufficient gestures of examination, touching,*
> *palping, pressing, etc.*

SEMINOLOGIST:
> Your husband's sperms are now of normal vitality,
> Mrs. Harding. Yet by the time they percolate here —
>
> *He pats her lower belly.*
>
> — a great proportion of them are dead. You would
> seem to be killing your husband's semen, Mrs.
> Harding: why is that?
>
> *There is no cruelty in his tone, merely a*
> *philosophical, mildly rebuking gentleness.*
> *ANNE can say nothing.*
>
> The medical profession has no answer in such a case.
> It may be that some form of chemical rejection is
> taking place —

ANNE: *clutching at a joyous straw*
> Something to do with antigens?

SEMINOLOGIST: *looking at her stilly, saying nothing, then*
> *speaking* This is a terra incognita of medical science.
> There is a broader possibility. In intercourse the
> vagina produces a self-protective acid. Sperms do not
> like this acid. The acid, therefore, not only helps
> prevent infection, it also acts as a goad to the sperms
> to hasten them on their way. Perhaps your vagina is
> producing too much acid, or too strong. Relax . . .
>
> *He comes away from her and goes over and sits*
> *behind his desk. Quietly, he speaks to himself.*
>
> So many good spermatozoa dead.
>
> *ANNE relaxes and sits up.*

ANNE:
> Massacre of the Innocents.

SEMINOLOGIST:
> Unjust, yes. Your doing, but not your fault.

ANNE:
> If I shove my fanny full of bicarb before we sex,
> would that do any good?

> > *She comes over to the SEMINOLOGIST at his
> > desk. He does not like being anticipated.*

SEMINOLOGIST:
> I was coming to the alkaline douche.

> > *He brings forward from his desk drawer a
> > package.*

> This is a little something of my own invention.
> Bicarbonate of soda is, yes, safe, and domestically
> available. But do remember you thereby expose
> your vagina to infection. So be moderate.

> > *He gives her the package.*

ANNE: *sitting down*
> Maybe we should just accept our infertility as our
> part played in easing an overpopulated world.

SEMINOLOGIST:
> And be content to leave the breeding to village yobs,
> clapped-out royalty and Papish slums? While the
> psychopaths that misgovern our globe make waste
> and slag of its sufficiency?

ANNE:
> I don't like to think of people in terms of absolute
> worth.

SEMINOLOGIST:
> Then start to think so. You know your Malthus as well
> as I do: the one inheritance Man is short in is Reason.
> Even if you and your husband look like the back
> ends of buses, you've more than an average share
> of Reason to bequeath. That is your duty to the
> world. If Man is to survive, he must evolve up out of
> his mythic mire; and soon. So tell your husband to
> keep up the cold water treatment and the diet; and
> you combine the posture and the alkali. We'll get you
> a bun in the oven for Hogmanay.

> *Briskly, he exits.*

> *COLIN becomes present on the bed.*

COLIN:
> Another seven old guineas, that sets us back.

> *ANNE undoes the packages. It is a comically
> flopping douche device.*

ANNE:
> And this, another two.

> *She squeezes the nozzle and makes a gurgling
> sound with her mouth. COLIN comes over to
> her. They play with the douche. Suddenly,
> however, as though they are afraid of losing
> their sexuality forever, their game becomes
> childish, desperate.*

> I wish we could get back to sex for kicks.

COLIN: *imitating the SEMINOLOGIST*
> "You are not one of those fortunates, Mrs. Harding,
> that can conceive with 'kicks': accept that. You
> might yet need recourse to my inseminator, a Heath
> Robinson device I've invented for ferrying live sperms
> through no-go areas."

The mood is suddenly broken. ANNE remembers
what the douche is for. COLIN speaks with a
new note of hardness. It is ill-suppressed.

Give fanny her gargle, then.

ANNE exits with the douche.

While I lie lashing up salacious thoughts of utmost
crudity to sustain my erection, my heart knocks like
a stone with the false effort. . . . Till you come from
the bathroom, cold as ice —

ANNE re-enters, gets on the bed and adopts the
"performing dogs" position.

ANNE:
To squat before my lord, my arse on high like Table
Mountain.

Speaking to the audience.

All grey in the dark.

All cats' arses are grey.

COLIN raises himself on his knees behind her.

COLIN:
And I must start upon her straightway. . . .

He reaches his hands beneath her.

And get my pint pulled up you straightway —

ANNE:
Being not sure how long or short the antacid effect
of the bicarb will last —

37

COLIN:

> To say nothing of the fact this bloody posture is
> giving me piles —

*Blackout. In the darkness, on the speakers,
the sounds of a slot-machine are heard —
rhythmic, dry, mechanical, luckless.*

The lights come up.

ANNE:

> Why can't we make like the amoeba?

COLIN:

> Split in two?

ANNE:

> Or freeze in a cyst, then explode in little hundreds.

COLIN:

> Defeat the object, wouldn't it?

ANNE:

> What is the object?

*They remain coupled, motionless, faces forward
towards the audience.*

COLIN:

> To think we were a year on the pill before we married.

ANNE: *speaking to the audience*
> Repeat on the thirteenth and fifteenth nights of the
> cycle. Two cycles. Five.

COLIN: *slowly withdrawing*
> Remembering always to come away carefully, not
> spilling any.

*He turns away from her and lies down, speaking
over his pillow to the audience.*

Sacrament, my arse. Four stages of a childless marriage. "Children?"

Speaking mildly.

"Not yet." "Children?"

Speaking with a slight rebuke.

"Give us time." "Children?"

Speaking gently, sadly.

"No." "Children?"

Speaking defiantly, as if, "Why should there be?"

No."

ANNE relaxes up into a Little Mermaid pose. She draws the blanket up around her and faces offstage.

ANNE:
"Try changing the wallpaper," they say. Aunts, mother-in-law, sisters. "It's nothing to do with the *function*," I tell them; "that part of it's all right."

VALERIE, a Young Married, appears behind her. She is pushing a pram and is obscenely pregnant. She speaks with a mixture of affected vulgarity and intellectual pretension.

VALERIE:
Try buying some different-coloured nighties, dear.

ANNE:
I've told you, Valerie: that part's in order!

VALERIE:

    Get him away, a romantic holiday, a second honey-
moon — or would it be the third or fourth, dear,
including those you had with him before you were
married?

ANNE:

    It's nothing —

VALERIE:

    George had his troubles, too. A warm climate's the
thing —

       *COLIN, being discussed behind his back, slinks
       unhappily off.*

ANNE:

    It's chemistry, Valerie. Not the sex, the chemistry.

VALERIE: *moving off*

    Perhaps he should take up football. On second
thoughts, perhaps not, knowing his past.

       ANNE is almost tearful.

ANNE:

    It's nothing to do with that! It's chemistry!

       She settles in her blanket.

Women. Young marrieds. Shriek to each other across
their prams. Joggle their dummy-stuffed spoils of
the sex war up and down. Trundle along their
suburban bellies bloated with the booty of the
bed. "How far are you on then, Doreen? Five
months? Oh, I'm six." Cows. The only function
they're up to, so they crack it high. Cows, cows.
They look at me. "*You* haven't pillaged your bread-
winner's basket in the dark when he thinks he's
polishing the top sheet with his arse; *you* haven't

ignited a brat; *you*'re no woman; *you*'re inadequate."
I get to hate my parasitic sex.

> *A GYNAECOLOGICAL SURGEON enters.*
> *He is smooth, well-groomed and impeccably*
> *dressed in a conservative fashion. He takes his*
> *place at his desk. He has in front of him a*
> *medical file on COLIN and ANNE which is*
> *quite full by now. COLIN and ANNE assemble*
> *themselves in front of him.*

GYNAECOLOGICAL SURGEON:
But in all these years of consultation, no one has
thought to confirm if you are in fact ovulating, Mrs.
Harding.

> *Speaking to the audience.*

Gynaecological surgeon, their last resort.

> *The GYNAECOLOGICAL SURGEON sits*
> *down. ANNE sits down opposite him; COLIN,*
> *at the desk end between them.*

No point in pumping your poor husband dry, if there
is no egg for him to fertilize.

> *He takes a slim packet from his desk drawer.*
> *It contains a thermometer.*

So, with your next cycle, you must begin a regular
taking of your morning temperature on waking,
entering it each day with a cross on this chart.

> *He brings out from his desk drawer a quarto*
> *buff envelope from which he takes out some*
> *blank temperature charts, for stage purposes*
> *somewhat larger than they might really be.*

> *COLIN and ANNE furtively glance at each*
> *other, reduced.*

41

If, round about your tenth day or so, the graph you are making suddenly dips, say five or six points of a degree, and the next day rises again by as much and a little more, you can normally assume ovulation has occurred. Whereupon, I recommend you two to initiate an orgy. After six months, if you have indeed not conceived before then, make an appointment to bring me the charts, so that I can see what ovulation pattern, if any, is suggested by them. It is helpful also if you ring the graph points on dates when intercourse has taken place.

He looks at the top letter in his file on them.

Bicarbonate of soda. Yes. Used in moderation, possibly quite helpful; though useless of course without ovulation, I think you understand that. Antacid effectiveness in the vagina, lasts quite some hours. You could douche yourself at leisure during the evening; earlier even.

He glances back down at the letter to take up the next of the points they have queried.

Posture. Circus dogs, you call it.

He shakes his head.

Unless you enjoy it that way. It makes mechanical sense, but has not, in my experience, significantly increased the chances of conception in a case like yours. One thing your letter does not make clear: your sperm counts, were they of motility only? Not of volume?

COLIN:
Not of volume. That I know of.

GYNAECOLOGICAL SURGEON:
I don't mean the quantity of the load, I mean its density in sperms. Your sperms can be the most

motile under heaven, but if they are few, say a mere fifty million per millilitre, then all the cold water in the world will not make you fertile.

COLIN:
I know the drill.

The GYNAECOLOGICAL SURGEON brings out of his desk drawer a long printed envelope that bulges slightly.

GYNAECOLOGICAL SURGEON:
Good. The more sperms you put into circulaton at any one time, the better your chances, I think you see that. The contents are self-explanatory: two forms, a sealable container. By post to the Path Lab, or drop it by: for this purpose, a time lag will not matter; even if all the sperms die in the post, it is merely a question of our counting the corpses.

COLIN takes the envelope. ANNE takes the thermometer and the charts.

If that, and these, are in order, I see no reason why the two of you should not be expectant by midsummer.

COLIN:
You will send the bill.

GYNAECOLOGICAL SURGEON:
Yes. And the charts and the thermometer together will come to an extra eighty pence.

He stands up quietly, ready to go.

Don't be despondent.

He exits. The lights change.

*ANNE goes over to the foot of the bed with
the charts, a pencil and the thermometer.
COLIN remains seated at the desk end. He
is halflit.*

ANNE:

Sixteenth of February, sixth day of cycle: ninety-
seven point nine, sexed.

*She traces her entries on the chart with the end
of the thermometer.*

Seventeenth of February, ninety-seven point seven.
Eighteenth of February, blank: faulty thermometer.
Ninth day of cycle, new thermometer, temperature,
ninety-eight. Ninety-seven point nine, sexed. Point
six. Point six. Blank — dropped thermometer.
Ninety-eight. . . . Sixteenth day of cycle, up:
ninety-nine point three. Point two, sexed; sore
throat and cold; point four. . . . Four, three, three.
. . . Twenty-eighth day of cycle, point eight again.
Period.

*COLIN bleakly looks across at ANNE's bowed
head. He feels hard in spite of himself. She
scans the charts as if she were looking for signs
of life there. She finds nothing. She turns and
speaks to the audience.*

They assure us it's neither's *fault*. Yet now it seems
because of his deficiency, now because of mine. That
gets at you. The combination of our chemistries, they
say. Yet now it seems his fault, now it seems mine.

*She sits down, demoralized by the charts.
COLIN, at the desk end, mimes speaking into
a telephone.*

COLIN:

I want only to find out if you have the *result* yet. . . .
But it has been rather a long time. . . . It was not a

44

motility test, madam, it was a density test. . . . Hell, the analysis must surely have been done by now, the figures must be somewhere. . . . I am not trying, madam, to tell Pathology their job; I merely wish you would credit other professions than yours with some scintilla of intelligence. . . . All I want to know. . . .

He pauses.

I appreciate you cannot tell me over the public line. Even if we could be sure the line was not tapped, I accept entirely your reason for that: but I am not asking for the result, I am merely trying to establish whether there yet is one, and when my doctor can expect to receive it.

He pauses once again.

I *am* aware your wheels rotate at an inflexible speed — God, this is England all over.

With bitter mimicry.

"We must preserve an empty mind." — Can you merely estimate roughly how long, from donation of sample, a man must wait for the alimentary process of your hospital to excrete a result? — For the Lord's sake, woman, it *is my sperm*. . . .

The GYNAECOLOGICAL SURGEON re-enters, simply, quietly. He sits at his desk. The lights change. He has a letter in his hands.

GYNAECOLOGICAL SURGEON:
Excellent. Perfectly satisfactory. Average, not more; but normally fertile. What more could you reasonably demand?

ANNE crosses the stage and sits down in front of him. She carries her charts with her. The GYNAECOLOGICAL SURGEON turns to her and looks at the charts.

GYNAECOLOGICAL SURGEON:
Now, here what have we? What are these?

ANNE hands him the charts. The GYNAECOLOGICAL SURGEON cannot seem to join them up. He looks at them and seems to find them scruffy. Suddenly, ANNE is as vulnerable as a pathetic slum child in front of an irascible teacher.

How do these connect?

ANNE tries to organize the charts. They become a muddle.

February. . . . Where is March?

ANNE and the GYNAECOLOGICAL SURGEON search in vain for March. COLIN and ANNE clumsily change places.

This blot: what happened here?

ANNE:
Thermometer broke.

GYNAECOLOGICAL SURGEON:
April. . . . Where is March?

COLIN watches the GYNAECOLOGICAL SURGEON with tense amazement and annoyance. The GYNAECOLOGICAL SURGEON points to the charts.

What are these diamonds?

ANNE peers at the charts.

ANNE:
>Pencil broke. It broke when I was doing a circle. For when we'd sexed. So I turned the circle into a diamond. Because of the scratch. So I turned them all into diamonds.

>>*The GYNAECOLOGICAL SURGEON holds up the charts for the audience to see. They are studded with diamond marks clustered in fours and fives midcycle and blank elsewhere.*

GYNAECOLOGICAL SURGEON:
>Whcre is March?

>>*It is found. The GYNAECOLOGICAL SURGEON re-arranges the charts.*

>Now we have a chronology.

>>*He waves ANNE to sit near him so that she can follow the charts.*

>Yes. . . .

>>*He ponders the charts.*

>A slightly erratic ovulation pattern; but it is there. Look, March; then July, this month. . . .

>>*He turns to COLIN.*

>You're still on the water?

COLIN: *suddenly stammering*
>Y—es. Two minutes every. . .

>>*The GYNAECOLOGICAL SURGEON turns back to ANNE.*

GYNAECOLOGICAL SURGEON:
>And the antacid douche?

COLIN:
Just as you t—. . . As you t—old us, yes . . .

There is an irrationally long pause.

GYNAECOLOGICAL SURGEON:
Well.

He pauses.

Well then, why aren't we conceiving? All that, in conjunction with these . . .

He points to the charts.

COLIN: *suddenly nervous, fatuous*
It's all rather like planning a moonshot.

The GYNAECOLOGICAL SURGEON ignores him.

GYNAECOLOGICAL SURGEON:
With all this, the odds now are, you should hit the jackpot before the end of the year. I frankly see nothing else I nor anyone can do, except leave it to Nature's blind will, with your rational assistance.

He collects the charts and clips them to their file.

You have approached the problem with realism and courage: I am sure your pertinacity will be rewarded.

The lights dim. The GYNAECOLOGICAL SURGEON exits.

COLIN: *turning and speaking "through" the audience*
Ay. In time to pick up our pensions on the way.

The lights go out. Soon, the shapes of COLIN asleep on the bed and ANNE, semi-cumbent

*beside him are seen. ANNE has the thermometer
in her mouth. She takes it out and reads it.
Soon, she begins to cluck like a hen. COLIN
wakes and begins to stir.*

What's up wi' *you*?

ANNE:
I've laid an egg. I've laid an egg!

COLIN:
Hang out the flags.

ANNE: *rising over him*
An innocent ovum has descended the Fallopian.
Come and get it.

COLIN:
I see. I'm in for a week of phallic martyrdom then,
am I?

*Blackout. In the darkness, on the speakers, the
sounds of a slot-machine are heard again.
Suddenly, there is a triumphant, cataclasmic
sound of money falling. The sound stops.
The voices of the DOCTOR and JENNIFER
calls across the dark stage to each other.*

DOCTOR:
Jennifer?

JENNIFER:
Doctor?

DOCTOR:
Mrs. Harding's urine sample: did you test it?

JENNIFER:
Yes.

49

DOCTOR:
What shall I tell her?

JENNIFER:
Tell her positive.

> *Organ music, orchestra and choir titanically burst forth. The first half dozen bars of Mahler's 8th Symphony, "Veni, veni Creator Spiritus," are heard. A pencilspot light illuminates the desk. It is draped, altar-like, with a white cloth and on top of it, centred, is a tall specimen container, chalice-like, filled with a straw-coloured liquid. The spotlight tightens until the specimen container glows like a Holy Grail. Brutally, in mid-paean, the music stops; the lights go out. There is silence, darkness.*
>
> *The second movement of the play follows as soon as practically possible.*

two

*A rapidly repeated piano-octave is heard:
Schubert's "Der Erikönig," the introduction —
clattering, empty and grim. In the darkness,
the specimen container, the cloth and the desk
are struck. The piano music fades before any
singer's voice is heard. Instead, stonechat- and
finch-song are faded up, intentionally lyrical,
a discreetly softcentred sound. The stage is lit
with warm sunlight. ANNE lies in her smock on
the naked ground. COLIN sits upstage of her
lazily stroking her belly. He is dressed in trousers
and has an open shirt. There is a tenderness
between the three of them — man, woman
and unborn child. COLIN tries to remember
the words of a poem, Traherne's "Salutation,"
but can manage only a halting garble.*

COLIN: *to himself*
    "What shall this be? That out of nothing comes. . . .
    Who, dust a thousand years . . . did in a chaos lie. . . ."

    *He puts his ear to ANNE's belly. As he caresses
    her, his sense of wonder broadens. It includes*

her. He waits a moment and then softly whistles a strain from "Brigg Fair." Suddenly, he turns to the audience and speaks.

COLIN:
So bloody English, this. All we need's a bit of Delius offstage.

The sound of a cuckoo is heard. If it makes the audience feel intellectually superior to the dramatist, so much the better.

ANNE: *not stirring*
There's a man in the South somewhere, has a cuckoo in a cage. He takes it out into his garden every spring, so that people can hear it and write to *The Times.*

COLIN's stroking of her begins to show sexual intent.

Not here, love —

COLIN:
Why?

ANNE:
People —

COLIN:
Who? Who's to see? No one comes up *this* hill anymore. . . .

ANNE: *in a mock Northern accent*
Officer wi' telescope.

COLIN:
Let him.

He is careful of ANNE's precious burden. He becomes more sexually purposeful.

ANNE: *shifting in sudden discomfort*
Trouble with being Lawrentian. Ants and . . . spines.
. . . Sorry, love, I'll have to pee first. This weight.

COLIN:
A heavy bladder is a stimulus to me.

ANNE:
Difference between us.

She moves away from him.

COLIN: *drawing her firmly down*
I'm damn glad we're *not* the amoeba.

> *They deepkiss. After a long moment, ANNE gets*
> *up and waddles off. COLIN remains behind,*
> *lying languorously on the ground. His gestures*
> *are discreet and private, fingers luxuriously*
> *stretched and hooking. They suggest the deep,*
> *still glory of his resurrected shaft, his reburgeoning*
> *testicles. He searches his memory for the line*
> *from the poem he was quoting earlier.*

Who shall . . . who shall he or she be . . . ? That out
of nothing comes. . . . A nothing: that all a sudden
. . . is. . . . Where there was empty darkness, a sudden
eye, seeing. . . . Sudden in emptiness, new-minted
limbs. Out of the dark silence, a forming tongue. . . .
Child. . . .

In an Ulsterish accent.

Jamie . . . or . . .

Again, in an Ulsterish accent.

Annie. . . .

> *There is silence. ANNE emerges from offstage.*
> *She is afraid to move. There is something wrong.*
> *COLIN turns sharply to her.*

ANNE: *quietly, hard*
No sex. Get me home. I'm passing these.

> *She thrusts into his sight, and the audience's, a*
> *white tissue in her cupped hands. It is black with*
> *clots of blood.*
>
> *There is a moment's pause. Shock goes off in*
> *COLIN like a deep mine exploding — he shows*
> *no other reaction. The lights go out; or, as the*
> *lights change, COLIN heavily brings home the*
> *things they have taken on their picnic.*
>
> *COLIN begins to make the bed. Its foot is*
> *towards the audience now. ANNE comes towards*
> *the bed. She is careful how she moves. She is*
> *dressed in a white nightdress now. She eases*
> *herself carefully onto the bed. COLIN exits.*
> *The DOCTOR from the opening scene enters. He*
> *wears a short driving coat and carries a black*
> *case. To one side, there is a chair on which he*
> *puts his jacket, his tie, etc.*

DOCTOR: *quietly*
How far are you on now, Mrs. Harding?

ANNE:
Three months.

DOCTOR:
Well; this is what we call a pregnancy at risk.

ANNIE:
What must we do?

DOCTOR:
> Stay in bed until forty-eight hours after the bleeding stops.

ANNE:
> It will stop?

DOCTOR:
> It'll have to stop some time. You haven't an inexhaustible supply.

> *Quietly, he exits.*

> *The lights change. COLIN enters and comes slowly downstage carrying a wicker wastebasket full of dark stained, bloody tissues.*

COLIN: *to the audience*
> And such blood. The clots of it, claret-colour, solid-soft. The child is lost. I don't mean I foresee that — we'll do everything mortal possible to prevent that. I mean, it is now that in the heart the loss takes place.

> *He is going to say something more, but decides not to. He turns and goes slowly upstage towards the bed, carrying the wicker wastebasket.*

> *The lights change. The DOCTOR comes in quietly. He wears a hat and carries the same black case. ANNE lies under the bedclothes, her head on a high pillow. She faces the audience. The DOCTOR rests his bag on the bed.*

DOCTOR:
> So what happened this time, Mrs. Harding?

ANNE:
> I lay as you said. The blood stopped. It dried. It came up brown and fibry. I saved you —

She makes as if she were going to bring out a bloody tissue from under her pillow. The DOCTOR gestures that there is no need for her to do this.

ANNE:

Thank God we got the spuds in before this happened.

DOCTOR:

Spuds in already?

ANNE:

He uses the Ulster calendar. In Patrick's Day, out Billy's day. Well, then I got up. I helped put in the tomato plants — well, *that*'s not strenuous.

COLIN: *returning, hovering with the wicker wastebasket*
I did the digging. I thought this year to water the soil very heavily at the start. Drive the roots down. . . .

He realizes he is chattering. He puts the waste-basket down by the bedside and exits.

ANNE:

In the night I felt wet. Blood again: red, bright; fresh. Bedrest. Dry again; forty-eight clear hours, then up again. *No* exertion this time. We're going out. I clean myself up. Blood again. Bed again. Dry again, up again, blood again; bed again. Doctor, that drug — there's a drug —

DOCTOR:

Our pharmacy shelves are full of that, we never prescribe it now. It seals you up. If you *insist*. . . . But if there's a good reason for a foetus to miscarry then miscarry we must let it. I know you have very much wanted this child, but you at least know now how you can conceive.

ANNE:
>I'm not that young.

DOCTOR:
>Nonsense.

ANNE:
>If it takes that long again I'll be over thirty. What you call it — an "elderly primate?" Superannuated ape.

DOCTOR:
>You won't find a good apple dropped from a tree. If that sounds like corny rural wisdom, it is nevertheless so. Things happen in their time.

ANNE:
>Doctor, what chance?

DOCTOR:
>Fifty-fifty.

ANNE:
>As bad as that?

DOCTOR:
>Try to keep calm. Stay in bed now.

>*He closes his bag and exits.*

>*COLIN enters, paler-faced than before. He wheels in a Variett-style table on which the height can be adjusted. On it are cereal in a dish, a boiled egg, bread, a coffee pot, some marmalade.*

>*It is a new day.*

COLIN: *with a slight hardness*
>How's the blood?

> *ANNE takes a clean tissue out from under her pillow, puts it under her bedclothes and pulls it out.*

ANNE:
> Started again.

> *She shows him the reddened tissue, almost flinching. His face is hard, still. He wheels the table so that it lies across her like a tray.*

COLIN:
> I'm not sure about the egg.

ANNE:
> What do you mean, "Not sure about the egg?" . . .

COLIN:
> Well, it's the second one. The first floated. Even this one tried to turn its beam end up.

> *ANNE sees that the salt is missing.*

ANNE:
> Salt.

COLIN:
> Sorry.

> *He goes to get it.*

ANNE: *shouting after him*
> I don't like the eggs from Clay Hall Farm, they taste of fish. God knows what they feed their poultry on.

> *She shakes some sugar on her cereal. COLIN comes in with the salt.*

> Darling, I'm sorry, you've forgotten the spoon.

COLIN:
Sorry.

He goes to get a spoon.

ANNE: *shouting after him again*
Why don't you get the eggs from Clink Farm?

She crunches into her cereal.

COLIN: *returning with a teaspoon*
Because Clink is out of my way.

He snatches his tie from the bedside chair and half ties it.

ANNE:
Oh, not that spoon, dear, for eggs; they stain. The Apostle spoons.

COLIN:
Sorry, I didn't think.

He goes to get another spoon.

ANNE: *shouting after him*
Well, how many times have you eaten an egg and not noticed what spoon you're using?

COLIN: *returning*
Judas, that do you? I'll go and have my own now --

The tray tilts over, spilling almost everything on it. ANNE screams and saves only the coffee pot and the egg. She holds these items, transfixed.

That's all I need.

ANNE:
Who didn't tighten the sodding screw?

*COLIN rights the tray and tightens the screw.
He restores what order he can to her breakfast.
The bread and butter has been loathsomely
dirtied on the floor.*

ANNE:
You're treading the cornflakes in —

COLIN:
Well, either you —

"Either you want me to tighten the table. . . ."

ANNE:
Well, don't. Oh, hell, there's milk on the blankets —

COLIN:
Well, I'm sorry — Use a tissue — A tissue! —

ANNE:
It'll come through to the sheets, love. I can't lie in
wet sheets. Sponge it off quickly — A sponge, love,
quickly! —

*COLIN exits to get a sponge. ANNE dabs at
the spilled milk with tissues. COLIN returns
with a sponge. They dab together.*

COLIN:
You'll need more milk now.

He goes to get her some more milk.

ANNE:
I'll eat the cornflakes dry, I'll drink the coffee black!

COLIN: *offstage*
Don't be silly.

*ANNE begins her breakfast. Offstage, an
unnecessarily loud cry of despair is heard
from COLIN.*

Oh no! No!

ANNE: *shouting*
What is it?

COLIN: *still offstage, furious*
Out. Out. Out! *Out!*

He pauses.

ANNE:
What's happened?

COLIN: *entering with a bottle of milk*
Excuse jug. Two pieces of news. First, the good.
The cat has puked.

He goes off again.

ANNE:
Feed her properly, she won't.

COLIN: *offstage*
She's perfectly fittingly fed.

ANNE:
You give her too much hardtack.

COLIN: *still offstage*
We're out of tins.

ANNE:
Get some on the way home then. Christ. Hardtack's
bad for them all the time. Hallucinogenic.

COLIN re-enters with a brush and dustpan.

COLIN:
What?

ANNE:

It blows their feline minds. Doctor was saying: three weeks on that hardtack and their cat was found cowering in front of a mouse.

COLIN: *brushing up the floor around the bed*
Now for the bad news. What I found in the vomit. A goldfinch head.

ANNE:

Oh no.

COLIN:

She's eaten one of the goldfinches from the tree. The other is fluttering around demented.

ANNE:

Oh no.

COLIN:

Stupid bitch of a cat. It'd be tolerable if she'd at least done it the honour of digesting it. Most beautiful songbird in Europe, what a waste. They chose our garden for their home. At their nesting they worked so hard. Collaborated so well. For their eggs and —

There is silence.

ANNE:

Better go and clean it up.

She takes a clean tissue and explores herself beneath the bedcovers.

COLIN:

I've not the time now.

His tie is half-tied. He snatches his jacket from the bedside chair.

ANNE:
It'll stink the place out, flies'll come in, it'll stain —

> *She brings out a bloody tissue from under the
> bedcovers.*

COLIN:
I'm supposed to be playing for Assembly this
morning.

> *He sees the tissue and offers her the wastebasket.*

Your egg'll be cold.

> *ANNE wipes her hand on the corner of her
> blanket.*

ANNE:
I don't want it.

COLIN:
Eat it. You're getting no lunch, you know that.

> *He exits with the brush and the dustpan.*

ANNE: *tapping the egg*
Egg smells funny.

> *She beheads the egg with a knife. Suddenly,
> she recoils convulsively from the egg and hurls
> herself to the floor. The audience sees her
> nightdress which is stained from her bleeding.
> Shuddering, she crouches, utterly turned over.*
>
> *COLIN re-enters, sees her on the floor and looks
> into the egg. He utters an amost inaudible choke
> of abomination and covers the egg with the
> nearest thing at hand. He stands, bottling his
> nausea and shock.*
>
> *ANNE speaks to herself.*

ANNE:
What am I trying to save? Some monster to be born, they'll take one look at —

COLIN stumbles away with the egg. The lights change. ANNE feels her belly, wondering what horror might be forming there.

Or a Mozart, Darwin? My will is blind. But is it itself willed, by some other will, that *sees*? That wills into being — Man's share of monstrosity or his share of light? Is it either of these? Or is the world's will wild? Without mercy, senseless? At the heart of things, what if there *is* no purpose, no logic, no love at all?

The lights change again and focus on the playing area downstage. ANNE dons a plain dressing gown and comes downstage. COLIN enters with a lounge chair, which he unfolds and erects. He is dressed as if he had come from school.

COLIN: *unsarcastically*
Have you thought how lucky we are? Unlike the Mrs. Seenys of this world: blessed by her bishop, no doubt, in whelping a degenerating line of brats she's neither intelligence, courage nor moral conscience to contraceive. And on our rates.

He brings the bedclothes down to the lounge chair.

Think how lucky. We know exactly *how* to click, and that's so damn roundabout a method, the thing itself really is "Love without Fear." Think of the rabbit. She ovulates every time she's entered. Homo sapiens is at least some way advanced on that. Perhaps you and I and others in our predicament are one stage even more evolved.

ANNE: *easing herself carefully into the lounge chair*
Right now I'd rather be an ammonite.

COLIN: *tucking her in*
Extinction hurts, too. We're wrong to patronize the
dinosaur, by the way. One of the kids was saying.
The dinosaur lasted five hundred times longer than
Man is likely to. It seems Man's last end, though, will
be the moral same.

> *He tidies the bedclothes.*

ANNE:
Out of step with his environment.

COLIN:
Worse than that. It seems there were tiny termites,
millions of them, eating their way up the dinosaur's
legs. His nerve system was so slow, out of touch with
his condition, the pain didn't reach the brain till all
his nethers were eaten away.

> *ANNE reaches out another bloodied tissue.*
> *COLIN automatically brings the wastebasket*
> *downstage.*

So what are *our* termites? What danger signal is the
human brain not getting?

> *He exits. VALERIE, the young married from*
> *earlier, breezes in.*

VALERIE:
Coo-ee, folks!

ANNE: *with mixed feelings*
Valerie?

65

VALERIE:
> The door was open.
>
> *She is no longer pregnant.*
>
> Anne, my love, you look so pale!
>
> > *Her cruelty throughout this scene is pure animal
> > — she deceives her better self that she is trying
> > to make ANNE feel welcome as a new member of
> > the suffering wife and mother club. She would be
> > ninety percent horrified if someone were to tell
> > her she were doing the cruel opposite.*
>
> I do hope Colin's cooking's not too awful.

ANNE:
> Oh, his hand's well in now. It *has* been weeks.
> Anyway, he didn't come straight from his mother's
> arms to mine.

VALERIE: *bringing a chair downstage and sitting on it*
> You must be ravenous, let me get you something.

ANNE:
> It's the life of Riley. Honest. Oh, a very *Protestant*
> Riley. . . . A curry or a carbonnade does two or three
> nights, on Fridays fish and chips from the van —

VALERIE:
> Nothing very Protestant about fish on Fridays — My
> poor thing, you're looking so pale! You mustn't let
> him frazzle you. I know men. He'll try to make you
> feel guilty because he has to knuckle to for once like
> a domestic martyr; he'll look at you accusingly
> because you're out of action bleeding your guts out.

ANNE:
> They're his guts as well in a way I'm bleeding out.

VALERIE:
> Don't let him. You need calm, peace of mind. I'll make some coffee.

> *She goes off to make some coffee.*

ANNE:
> He was like that a bit at first. But he had it all to do: house, cooking, nursing, garden — examination term. He's very organized now though: real Time-and-Motion. "Stop and think." Before he does anything "Stop and think." I've never seen him so still.

> *Offstage, a jug crashes.*

VALERIE: *offstage, her voice tearful*
> Oh, Anne, I'm so sorry. I'll pay you for it — No, I insist. Even if I have to scrub floors.

> *She appears with a fragment of a blue and white Cornish pottery jug.*

> I do hope it wasn't sentimental. It says, "Tintangle." Was that where you had one of your honeymoons, dear?

ANNE:
> That. Was already in his collection when I joined it. I think Tintagel was where he began drafting that big play of his; the one no one ever did.

VALERIE:
> Ah. His writing days. Old times.

> *She exits with the fragment of the jug.*

ANNE:
> Heard about that man arrested in Brum the other day? Blowing bubbles in the street? He got fined. For "obstruction." I want this previous little bastard, if he lives, to be a blower of bubbles, Christ, I do.

She speaks quieter, more and more to herself.

ANNE:

Oh, I don't know. You bring a kid up anarchist, he ends up joining the police. How do you bring up a spirit to be free? Shove his tongue up the anus of authority and trust to his instinct for revolt? Manipulation, that. Hell's teeth, why hang my hang-ups round the necks of the unborn?

She addresses her belly.

Bloodbeast. Take over the graveyard in your own good time and your own right. If you see our values have failed us, cack on our graves.

VALERIE returns with two coffees in cups on a tray.

VALERIE:

Look pleased to see me.

ANNE: *meaning no slight*
I'm pleased to see anybody, stuck like this.

VALERIE:

Thank *you*!

*They drink their coffee. There is a pause.
VALERIE begins to speak in a new tone — a
"we women can't win confidence."*

Speaking of bastards.

She pauses.

You're not the only one with troubles. *I*'m over*due*. I shouldn't be saying this to you in your condition, but what I've been going through! — I don't *want* it, Anne; I can't have it; well, I can't, can I? how can I?

It isn't George's, it's Fred's. Oh, I *know*. . . . What's so awful, we've only slept together once this cycle —

ANNE:

You have it easy, all you have to do is *sleep* together! . . .

VALERIE:

But isn't it rotten, such rotten luck, Anne? Oh, Anne, love, it's so *horrible*. . . .

She bursts into tears.

Here are you two, suffering all this time to get one even started, and you're not able to keep it in; here's yours truly racking her tiny brain how to get hers out on the scrapheap in time. It's a pig of a world, so unjust, I can't tell you how sorry for you both I am: I wake up thinking how pale you both are, your pale faces, and you were so healthy before you married and so *happy*. . . . God, in the old days, Colin —

She forgets her tears.

— on that Lambretta — looking so brown —

COLIN enters, utterly unselfconsciously tying a woman's apron about his waist.

COLIN:

Ah, *here's* the tray —

VALERIE: *seeing the apron and shrieking*
Colin! Colin! I never thought to see the day!

COLIN:

What? Oh this.

69

He camps slightly with the apron — to trap her.
VALERIE utters a camp giggle. ANNE wryly
watches.

COLIN:
Yes, you *would* think it funny. I just happen to be
weird: I don't see how it is manlier somehow to let
one's clothes get wet.

He takes the tray and leaves the cups.

VALERIE: *shouting after him*
I didn't say anything about your not being virile,
Colin! Lord, how should I know?

She turns to ANNE, resuming her "we women
can't win" tune.

God, the trouble I had carrying Jason. *He* simply
re*fused* to be born. George was driving me over level
crossings, foreways and backways; the little bugger
simply *refused* to be born. Christ, when he did come,
such a relief, my dear: to be able to see your toes
again.

Something — a sound from the kitchen perhaps
or a perceptible withdrawal suddenly in ANNE
— makes VALERIE feel redundant.

Ah well. When you're up and about again, my dear,
you must come and have tea with me and the
children and we'll have a jolly old cow.

She stands and whispers in ANNE's ear.

Don't let him *frazzle* you, dear.

Calling as she goes.

By-ee!

*COLIN emerges. He jabs his thumb in
VALERIE's departed direction.*

COLIN:
When my mother was in the Royal Victoria having
that breast off, there was an old biddy from
Ballymacarrett sat up on high pillows opposite her
all the day, dangling . . .

He gestures.

. . . her full pair over the bedclothes. For cruelty, of
all the sexes, women are the worst.

He kisses ANNE, takes the cups and goes.

*ANNE, questioningly, feels her belly. She is
troubled. COLIN re-enters and sits on the chair.
He is still aproned. He speaks quietly.*

I never know what I'll find instead of you when I
get home. And at night: I sleep deeper than hell, yet
the slightest shift of you, I'm full sharp awake —

He pauses.

ANNE:
It wakes me, too, the blood.

COLIN:
My frazzle didn't make you any better. My frazzle
at the beginning is part of the fault of it.

ANNE: *to disabuse him*
I lost a little at the *second* month.

*Each of them is suddenly conscious of their
irremediable personal separateness.*

COLIN:
My anxiety made you worse. That's why I slowed up. Anyway, we can have wrong things invested in a child.

ANNE:
I know.

COLIN:
If he or she is born, then he or she is born. If it is a matter of your will only, he shall be born. It's easy for me. I've everything to do. You've nothing but to lie, lie, willing.

He reaches over to pat her belly. She stays his hand.

ANNE: *pausing*
I think it's died.

There is a long silence.

ANNE's voice is helpless.

There isn't the little flutter any more.

COLIN: *speaking at last*
Maybe it's just lying quiet a while. They do that, don't they?

He pauses.

Or playing possum. Perhaps he's realized, it's life or death: so he just daren't rock the boat — too — vigorously . . .

He pauses, then begins to speak briskly.

What simple task for you can I find, won't overtax your inferior domestic female mind?

He exits and re-appears with a bowl of washed
spuds, a saucepan, a spudbasher and a newspaper
for the peelings.

For thick wife: "Put ze rett triankles in ze rett boxes,
and ze green ones in ze green boxes."

ANNE seizes the spudbasher in her fist and
makes a stone age, idiot gesture. COLIN sits
on the chair beside her and they begin peeling
potatoes.

That Eysenck book, by the way. The know-your-own-
IQ one. I found a mistake. Well, not a mistake so
much: an omission. Very revealing. He has a
question: "Fill in ze missink letters. H,E, blank,
I,T,A, blank, E."

ANNE thinks; does her idiot act.

ANNE:
Artichoke.

They peel on a few moments.

COLIN:
No, think.

He writes with his fingers on the newspaper.

H,E, blank, I,T,A, blank, E.

ANNE studies the newspaper, as if the letters
were present there.

ANNE: *speaking at last*
I can do the picture ones, I can't do the word ones.
I'm illiterate, I can't spell English, I didn't do any
Latin at school.

73

COLIN: *pausing, then speaking in an exaggerated Ulster tone* H.E. Blank. I.T.A. Blank. E.

ANNE: *immediately*
Heritage.

COLIN:
Heritage. So I thought. But not Our Father Eysenck. For him, the word is Hesitate. Let us anatomize the Eysenckian universe. The planet Heritage does not so much as flicker in it. For Eysenckian man inheritance does not exist — except as a congenital tic. In behaviourist Utopia we do not belong, we conform; we do not inherit, we obey. In Eysenckania, we each look vertically up, and up alone, parched lips straining for one normalizing eucharistic drop from the chalice of Paternalist Authority. Who does not crave so, electric treatment shall put right. Heritage, my arse. He-si-tate. To stutter to stammer to stumble to *be unsure, that*, in the Eysenck cosmos, is our determined role.

ANNE:
Perhaps he just forgot.

COLIN:
The man who'd speak from Sinai has no business "forgetting."

ANNE: *gently*
Did you switch 'oven on?

> *COLIN has forgotten to switch the oven on. He exits to do this. ANNE quietly moves the newspaper and her peelings down a bit and lets her hand rest on her belly. She is uneasy. From under her pillow on the lounge chair, she takes out a clean tissue. Cautiously, she puts it beneath her blanket. She brings the tissue out. There is no visible stain on it, yet there is something there she does not like. She looks*

*carefully at the tissue, then smells it. She folds
the tissue and puts it in her dressing gown
pocket. She will show the DOCTOR. She begins
to peel potatoes again, but she is uneasy. After
a moment, she tries to steepen the headrest
behind her. Without knowing, she jerks it too
far forward before resting it carefully back at
what she thinks is a new angle. She does not
lean back immediately, but brings the newspaper, peelings and potatoes back into reach.
Then, she leans back. The headrest falls flat,
she with it. After a moment, she sees she will
have to ease herself off the lounge chair to
adjust the headrest. Clumsily, not daring to
bend her body, she manoeuvres herself stiffly,
sideways off the lounge chair. Her foot tips
the spudbowl over and the spuds and the water
spill. She collapses onto her knees amid the wet
and the dirt — heavy, crumpled, breathless.*

COLIN comes in quietly and sees her.

COLIN: *annoyed that she didn't call for help*
You hopeless woman.

He starts to clear the mess.

ANNE:
I'm all wet.

COLIN:
You've coggled the bowl, I'm not surprised you're
wet.

ANNE: *without turning to him, putting her hand on her
belly*   No, *here* I'm wet.

There is a pause.

My waters have broken.

She turns her face to him. There is a still moment.

A gentle, heavy-sized AMBULANCE DRIVER enters. He unfolds a stretcher and lays it out on the floor between the lounge chair and the bed.

COLIN goes to collect what things ANNE will need in the hospital. There is no flap about him, his actions are all smooth.

AMBULANCE DRIVER: *speaking in a deeper rural accent than the DOCTOR had, perhaps Birmingham-tarnished* Now don't you worry, dear. We'll get you there quick as we can. By the smooth road. We know all the bumps in the Country, don't you worry.

Gently, he helps ANNE onto the stretcher.

This lady now sees, for the first time she fully sees: she'm in danger of death. Some'at about our sympathy, in how familiar we are with her condition, in how serious and careful it makes us of her, strikes the scale from her eyes.

He brings a red blanket to spread over her.

From her bed, from her room, from her little house now we bring her, gentle, gentle on the stretcher. . . . Easy then, Albert. Easy. . . .

He draws the stretcher backward, ANNE's head first, towards the bed, which is a moveable rostrum.

Out to the ambulance. . . . Ambulance: common enough thing, you say. But to her, to this woman, this ambulance is the valley of the shadow, that sad little shadow through which one in five British mothers pass.

He climbs backwards up onto the rostrum, as
though he is stepping back into an ambulance.
The stretcher is raised, on a slope. ANNE is
displayed to the audience like a straw man.
She is undignified, helpless.

Don't she look like a witch, eh, on her ladder? Or a
Jewess, trussed on her tray for the boiler? *Her* turn
now: where others have gone, now she. What other
people have, now hers to suffer. Alone.

His face is next to hers. He speaks to the
audience.

Look, a tear. Swells up out of nothing in the socket
of her eye. The salt drop from the gland: fills, bulges,
quivers. Makes her look so stupid. Weak face, stupid,
helpless; slack jaw, so helpless, stupid. It tears your
heart in two for pity, and your right hand itches up
to strike that stupid face.

He speaks to ANNE — utterly straight and
without pretence.

There, dear, lie still. We'll get your things together,
don't you worry.

Speaking to the audience once again.

Beginning to shed; so shove her in gentle.

He shoves the stretcher along the rostrum into
the darkness.

Close the doors.

COLIN enters slowly, still wearing an apron.
With deliberation, he clears away the potatoes,
the lounge chair — they will not be needed now.
He goes off and comes back on, not hurrying.
While working so, he speaks to himself.

COLIN: *speaking quietly*

Now think. Think how this happens from some good
cause. If a bomb or a soldier had done it, you could
be bitter. Think, how it can have some — rightness.
The way of nature. Yet, was it in the way of nature,
what we did? Lend her a helping hand? Nature might
— take unkindly to our — "help." I rescued a shrew
once, from the cat: yet the shrew ran straight off the
shovel, into a drain. The struggling in the water; the
sound of the little blind thing struggling in the water.
"Helped." It is true: what happens to us in the world,
bears no resemblance to "morality." Yet, from that —
inequity, might there not be a lesson to be learned?
We are so near the letters, how can we see the word?

There is a silence.

In nature there is no annihilation. The dead are eaten.
What remains rots down in corruption. In corruption
itself murmur the bubbles of rebirth. Even what was
burned, from ashes the fields are fertilized. For all
that: however a cosmos might absorb calamity,
extinction's final — for the thing extinct.

*The lights change. A NURSE comes in with
white sheets and pillows. She transforms the
rostrum into a hospital bed. ANNE enters
slowly, wearing a dazzling clean white nightdress. She is helped into bed and lies facing
the audience. The NURSE raises ANNE's
head on the pillows, then exits. ANNE lies
listless. She talks to the audience.*

ANNE:

We thought we'd saved it. The cervix contracted, it
almost closed. One of the doctors had hobnailed
boots on his fingers: whenever he examined me —

Her breath fails in remembered pain.

I'd only to *see* it was him on the wards, I'd start to

bleed. . . . But we thought we'd saved it. They even told Colin: "Come in with her clothes tomorrow, she'll be all right." But when he came with the suitcase, "We're sorry," they said, "she's had a bad night; she must stay a while longer." One morning they rang him. "Your wife's going down to the theatre," they said. He saw what that meant. "I see," he said, "for the scrape, you mean." "Scrape?" they said. "Well, if we've lost the baby —" he said. "Baby?" they said. "What baby?" They looked in the records. "It *is* Mr. Harvey?" "Harding," he said. "Oh. Harding. Oh no, Mr. Harding, oh I *am* sorry, oh no, Mrs. Harding's perfectly all right —" He was always last out of visiting. One night, five minutes after he left, I wanted a crap. I called for the bedpan. But it wasn't a crap. It was just as easy as a crap. Easier. Plop, it was out —

She screams.

Nurse!

> *There is darkness. The lights come up — a blinding white light. The sheets, the pillow behind ANNE's head are a blinding white. COLIN comes in quietly, bringing a chair. He sits at her bedside, in his hand a pathetic bunch of fresh wild flowers that he has picked for her, a share in the spring she is missing.*

COLIN:
The ditches are white with stitchwort.

He shows her the flowers.

Herb Robert. Cranesbill. Campion.

He gives her the flowers.

ANNE: *too listless to take them*
There were two. Two babies. One came, then I was
unconscious; then the other, it woke me in the night.
I said, "Is it a boy?" "Nothing," she said, "it's only
clots." But it was a baby. I know it was. There were
two. They were twins. One must have gone wrong,
you see. One must have been wrong from the start.
So it died in the womb, it brought them both out, the
good one with the bad.

She is motionless.

The nurse won't tell me. I only want to know it
wasn't a monster. Or that it *was* a monster. I don't
know what it is I want to know.

She pauses.

They're in the fridge. They take them to the end of
the ward and — put them in the fridge. In the next
ward you can hear the good ones crying, the ones that
have been born. You have to have the different gyny
wards together, that's only sense. . . .

COLIN:
Next ward's where we'll be. Next time.

ANNE: *still motionless, seeming not to hear him*
I said to the doctor, I won't go through all this again.
Oh, he's a patronizing bastard, the nurses queue up
to kiss his arsehole — He's only a *doctor*! I won't
go through this again, I told him: bugger this for a
tale. Next time I start to bleed I'll go down to my
husband's school and hire the trampoline.

COLIN:
Next time we'll be in there. This happens to one
couple in five first time. We'll be in there next time.

ANNE: *still motionless, her mind no longer wandering*
He said — he said — "There isn't going to be a next time, Mrs. Harding. I'm sorry. We have had to take the womb away."

She pauses.

"I'm sure your GP will recommend you for adoption."

There is a silence.

ANNE suddenly buries her head in COLIN's breast.

I'm sorry, love, I'm sorry —

COLIN: *stunned*
Why "sorry?" —

ANNE mutters something indistinct — about giving him children. He can find nothing to say except "No.... No...."

No.... No....

He means, "Stop saying you're sorry."

ANNE mutters something indistinct again — about wanting to have his *children.*

No, no.... Stop being so Arab. It's not "giving children," it's having. *Our* children, not mine. No. No.

ANNE: *in a constrained movement, orchestrating her pinned anguish* I can see the smoke. From the incinerator. Burning my womb! —

They remain motionless, silent. COLIN speaks at last.

COLIN: *very quietly*
Gone then. Gone. Gone. We must do what we can
with what remains. All that, is gone.

> *ANNE utters one nigh-inaudible gasp of grief.
> She shakes bitterly, then is silent. COLIN
> speaks in a deathly quiet.*

Gone.

> *They remain motionless, silent.*

> *Blackout.*

three

*Chill pianissimo music is heard, the epilogue to
Vaughan Williams' 6th Symphony — spare,
groping, desolate. In the darkness, the set is
struck. The stage is bare except for two chairs.
The music fades and a lifeless light comes up.
A SOCIAL SERVICES OFFICER sits on one
of the chairs. He is in his mid-thirties, compassionate and quite smooth. His suit is a
clerical grey. On his crossed legs he carries a
set of duplicated notes. His chin rests on a steeple
of his hand and he eyes his audience perceivingly,
first this couple, then that, as if they were
nervously sitting in front of him in a semicircle.
Near him, slightly upstage and out of alignment
with him is the AREA ADOPTIONS OFFICER,
a woman in her early thirties, smart, conventional, attractive. She carries a clipboard which
she holds in her lap. She discreetly watches this
couple, then that, noting a reaction here, a
giveaway gesture there. Once or twice, she will,
all but imperceptibly, make a brief mark on her
list of names while the SOCIAL SERVICES
OFFICER speaks.*

SOCIAL SERVICES OFFICER: *gently, absolutely, enshrin-*
ing a hardness, he must prepare his hearers for the
worst We, in the Authority, realize you come to us
as a last resort. We accept that. You have discovered
for yourselves there is no "host of unwanted
children" awaiting adoption: abortion laws, more
tolerant attitudes to illegitimacy, have seen to that.
Private and religious agencies are in abeyance; all
over the country the lists are closing. This application
you have lodged with us is thus virtually your last
chance for parenthood of any kind. If then, as I
speak, you are furtively assessing these other couples'
chances with us against your own, that is only
understandable. For you know this is not a matter
of rivalry so much between you; yet you also know —
if not, you are not ready for adoption — to adopt
means, not to find a child you think suits *you*, but
for us, the County, to find a home we think right
for the child. Thus, in the nature of things, we can
never say yes to you all. Even those of you brave
enough to offer a home to a child of other or mixed
race, or to a child in some way handicapped, we shall
almost always have to turn away. There are not the
children. Sad then though your path has so far been,
it may yet lead to further sadness. We share that
sadness. You come to adoption because you have had
to accept that natural parenthood is a common,
human heritage from which you are shut out. You
have had to rethink parenthood; perforce matured,
into seeing a possible child of yours, not as a product
of your self, but as an infant person already possessed
of his or her own history, bringing it with him,
absolute in his own right. You have learned, a hard
way, that in true parenthood there is no fantasy, no
self-extension, no fond notion of vertical inheritance
of what you think is best in *you*: you leave such
fatuous hopes behind, evolving perhaps towards
something more like a parenthood of tomorrow.
For some sociologists tell us, that tight little knot of
domestic mirrors we call the Family, is a unit Man
might now need to question and reject; that the

family of tomorrow might possibly be something broader, more mixed — horizontal; fraternal. Many children, many parents, in one extended family. If so, then you who have thought and fought your way through a peculiar disappointment and peculiar grief to some such — forgive me — new *conception* of father- and motherhood, perhaps stand today more firmly on this threshold of tomorrow than those conventionally blest. But. If you have had cause for a painful self-search before, I must warn you there is more to come. You would not feel safe in committing yourselves to a child of whom you knew nothing: still less can we hazard a child to a home of whose history, values and likely future we had not found out all we reasonably could. You must be prepared for prolonged and deep investigation: medical, professional, financial; marital. You will flinch from this inquisition; at times feel laid out on our slab just once too often. Appreciate our reasons. Nor is it pleasant for us, submitting a man's or a woman's deepest motives to dissection. Our Area Officer, Mrs. Jones, who shares this casework, will endorse me on this.

The AREA ADOPTIONS OFFICER makes discreet minimal acknowledgement of his remark.

Be warned. Expect little. Even if in the end we find you would make a most excellent couple for our list, it might still be most unlikely such a child will become available to us, as you will suit. In such a case, we prefer to get your disappointment over and done with straight away. Our reasons, however, for not accepting you, whatever they are, we never give. Painful though it is, to be found unsuitable and left wondering for ever why, we find that on balance it is safer for you to be left in the dark. We marvel constantly at the courage would-be adoptive parents show. You begin to see now, how much you really need.

*The light shrinks. The SOCIAL SERVICES
OFFICER and the AREA ADOPTIONS
OFFICER exit quietly.*

*From the darkness, pale, naked but for a pale
blue pair of briefs, comes COLIN. In his hand,
he carries his black leather shoes, his socks
rolled up inside them; over his arm, he carries
a vest, a white linen shirt, a black tie, a light
cardigan of fawn wool, his black funeral suit.*

COLIN: *as he slowly dresses*
Last time I wore this, was over in Ireland too. Some
country. Some "Mother." Only cause can bring us
flying back till her is death. . . . Poor Uncle Tommy.
"Fine fella of a mahn." To end in pieces. What sort
of son am I, to such fine fathers? White sterile son,
dead branch of the tribe. . . . No. No. All that's
behind me. Progenitive fantasy, all behind me. For
fatherhood I was not made. Nature was wise, she
cast me from the start: dead seed, best fix to mix
with excrement — ashes to ashes.

Sarcastically.

But I knew better. "I knowed better." I would
be a "mahn." A "father." With cold water and
bicarbonate of soda, chart, calendar and clock —
"Hi, oul' bitch, Nature," I said, "I'll worst ye yet!"
If I had been content —

He pauses.

Content. . . .

He sees the truth of it.

Content . . . my wife would have her womb this day.
Application for Adoption. Name, birthdate, address,
profession, religion — none; average income, size of

house, medical history — likelihood suddenly to die;
biographical remarks —

Self-mocking.

I wrote them half a novel there. . . . Two independent
referees outside the family. . . . First interview, the two
of us, here. Next interview, there, myself alone: "Mr.
Harding, how genuinely motivated for parenthood do
you think you are?"

*He is dressed now. He sits on the chair, his black
suit emphasizing his pallor, his longing.*

A child to come to us, absolute in his own right, his
own inheritance, free of ours. . . Real child, a
daughter, a son, real. . . . Real flesh, real self, real
person, real . . . to come to us, sidelong. . . . Not
down from us, but out, across the world, to us . . .

*After a moment, he gets up and goes into the
darkness. The AREA ADOPTIONS OFFICER,
Mrs. Jones, comes in with a file. She moves the
chair to a new position. ANNE, pale, nervous,
wearing a drab camel coat, comes in and sits
down on the other chair, almost facing her. She
takes off her coat. Her frock is a bloodred
shock, as though the blood on the tissue had
grown through the stain on her nightdress to
become all of her. The AREA ADOPTIONS
OFFICER's tone throughout is utterly unreveal-
ing, objective; quiet, compassionate, but
searching. She hardly takes her eyes off ANNE
at all.*

AREA ADOPTIONS OFFICER:
    Mrs. Harding. How strongly do you want to become
    a parent?

ANNE:
    I think our history answers that.

87

AREA ADOPTIONS OFFICER:
> You have shown remarkable perseverance. When I
> spoke to your husband, he said how much he admired
> your willpower when you lay there — how did he
> put it? — "willing your foetus to stay in place."
> I thought he, too, had from the beginning shown
> quite frightening willpower. Why do you think he
> did so?

ANNE:
> For fatherhood.

AREA ADOPTIONS OFFICER:
> Simply that?

ANNE: *thinking*
> For Colin, fatherhood isn't a simple thing. Whenever
> I come to an interview I end up talking about him. It
> was the same when I was trying for the stage: at
> auditions, we ended up talking about him. He used
> to write plays.

AREA ADOPTIONS OFFICER: *with the faintest wintry
humour* We talked about you last week.

ANNE:
> Yes. When he got home, I asked him how it went.
> "Lousy," he said, "I reckon I talked our child away."

> *There is a silence, then the AREA ADOPTIONS
> OFFICER speaks.*

AREA ADOPTIONS OFFICER:
> How do you think he would react if we were to turn
> down your application, knowing that with it there
> almost certainly goes your last chance?

> *ANNE thinks, then speaks.*

ANNE:

> He'd be very bitter. Then he'd accept. What else?
> We'd both accept. Then move on.

AREA ADOPTIONS OFFICER:

> Away?

ANNE:

> Oh no. I mean, if we're not to be parents, move on
> to what we *can* become.

AREA ADOPTIONS OFFICER: *pausing*

> What do you think is your husband's worst fault?

ANNE:

> Pigheadedness. It's sort of — Protestant integrity, but
> it comes over as pigheadedness.

AREA ADOPTIONS OFFICER:

> When he discovered he had no future as a writer, he
> didn't resist that. He turned away and started another
> life.

ANNE:

> Thousands do that. I did that.

AREA ADOPTIONS OFFICER:

> If we were to refuse you, what would your reaction
> be?

> *ANNE has pondered this already.*

ANNE:

> It would all seem part of the evolving pattern.

> *She sees that the AREA ADOPTIONS OFFICER*
> *would like her to amplify this remark.*

> When our careers collapsed, his and mine, we began
> to read it as a sort of message, if you like: that we
> ought to — take a different road. We came out here;

we went back to teaching, for which we'd both been trained; we became rural and domestic. Soon the idea of children became important. Well, you know what happened about *that*. So. If we're turned down, it'll be pretty conclusive this was a wrong road, too.

There is a long silence.

AREA ADOPTIONS OFFICER:
How strong do you think your marriage is?

ANNE thinks about this.

What do you think is the greatest threat to it?

ANNE: *speaking at last*
If one knew *that* . . .

AREA ADOPTIONS OFFICER:
Your husband's answer to this question was . . .

She takes a brief glance at her notes.

"When the earthquake happens, the buildings that survive are the ones that swayed." How do you think he means, your marriage could sway? His rather unorthodox sexuality, you think because of that?

ANNE:
I don't think he meant the *marriage* could sway. I think he meant about people rolling with the punches that Nature gives them.

AREA ADOPTIONS OFFICER:
Yet you say he is pigheaded.

ANNE: *candidly*
He's learning.

She pauses.

Anyway. I don't think his sexuality is unorthodox.
His acknowledgement of it might be. We have to tell
you these things.

AREA ADOPTIONS OFFICER:
That he can consciously feel for his own sex, do you
think that threatens your marriage?

ANNE:
I feel safer.

AREA ADOPTIONS OFFICER:
Safer?

ANNE:
Safer than if he had a roving eye for other women.
Anyway, I've told him. If he has to have a bit of the
other sex once in a while, just be sure to come back
clean. It's how he's made; he has only one life.
Likewise me. If I *have* to succumb to the milkman,
he says, "Just not in *our* bed." It's a joke but . . .
a grain of truth. If that shocks you, I'm sorry.

AREA ADOPTIONS OFFICER:
It doesn't *shock* me —

ANNE:
We don't abuse each other's liberality. Anyway, men
with open homosexual emotions are supposed to
make good fathers. It's just a rotten consequence of
natural logic so few of them get the chance.

AREA ADOPTIONS OFFICER:
Is your marriage satisfactory, Mrs. Harding?

ANNE:
Bed, you mean?

AREA ADOPTIONS OFFICER:
Among other things.

ANNE:
Not always. In fact, it's rather bad just now. The
tension all this has put us under. And the fact that I
shall never conceive does — to begin with anyway —
make a difference. He's not the great greasy bullock
of my dreams, what woman's husband is? It's probably
better to find your man tolerable company for fifty
years than be hooked on his cock. I don't even like
my husband all the time: but for good or ill, he's
in my belly now.

AREA ADOPTIONS OFFICER: *at last*
What do you think you have to offer a child, Mrs.
Harding?

ANNE thinks a long time, then speaks.

ANNE:
Nothing. Specific. Just what we'd have to offer
children of our own. I can't think of anything. Just
a — share in living.

Blackout.

*In the darkness, the audience hears airport
sounds — the sound of an aircraft landing. The
set is struck. The rostrum is brought back on
and in front of it are placed two chairs — the
front seat of a van. Ding-dong. The voice of an
airport announceress is heard, "BEA announce
the arrival of flight number BE four-two-five
from Belfast." This message is repeated. The
sounds of an airport corridor are heard — many
people trooping. The aircraft sounds fade. Two
car doors slam. The sound of an ignition is
heard; a car pulls away. The lights come up.
COLIN and ANNE sit in the van; he, a passenger
in coat; she, by implication, driving.*

COLIN: *trying for the thousandth time to realify the horror to himself* They all stood, paralyzed. Someone had said, "There's a second bomb, keep away." But after a minute, they could bear the tension no longer; they all rushed forward. In. They say the scene that met their eyes was — unspeakable. Pieces of people, hunks of unrecognizable torn flesh; pathetic items of shopping, clothes, schoolbooks; a boy's head. The nethers of a pregnant woman, skewered on a busstop shaft. Spatters of digest, shite and half-shite. Tissue, bone, deep slimes of blood; a knot of intestines slowly sliding down a wall. Atrocious anagram of people coming home. A Swedish photographer, had Auschwitz, Korea, the Congo, Vietnam in his belt, had to be carried away hysterical and vomiting. Somewhere in that, Uncle Tommy had died. To that conclusion, his days had been bringing him all along. What call have we, to be appalled? What claim have we, on moral repugnance? What's so especially obscene about this sort of bomb? That it comes from below? Delivered by citizen to fellow-citizen, not sent long-distance through the air above? Local, and small enough, to class as an outrage: not global, and technocratic enough, to rank as policy? Just ends do not justify violent means, we are told. Except of course on a governmental scale. Ireland as ever brings that logic remorselessly home where it belongs. To us. And here, by God, only beginneth the lesson. "So why did ye stay across the water so long?" Aunt Annie said. "Ye know ye could have come live wi' us at any time, why did ye not come here?" she said, "wi' us?" I said, "Because I was afeared. Truth to tell, Aunt Annie, I was afeared to come. Forbye, because I am so torn." "Between what?" Between the baker's halfdozen wrongs of this all. Torn, I tried to tell her, torn wondering where best — no, not where best; where at all we go now. "Aunt Annie" — my heart was in my mouth as I said it — "we've known from Year One our old North of Ireland had to go some time." As a child, every

August the 12th, I marched with the Prentice boys
round Derry Walls. The Fenians in Bogside would
save their filthiest rubbish to burn that day, so the
smoke from their chimneys'd dirty our shirts. And I
really believed: that, was a moral disposition of the
world. Oh, this side of the water I might wonder a
little what life was like below those walls — and
there are Bogsides here, too. I have always known
trouble would come in that city. When the riots
broke out, I was disturbed: I began to wonder. Awful
to say, but only these bombs have made me really
think. If an undertribe can commit themselves to
such atrocity, there must be some terrible misery they
are trying to communicate. And our . . .

He searches himself deeply for these words.

. . . inequity . . . monopoly of things . . . self- . . .

*This last word he almost fails to find. "Self-
satisfaction," no. He tries again.*

Self- . . .

*He still cannot find the word. At long last, after
appalling self-search, he says . . .*

. . . certainty. . . .

He pauses.

Self-certainty and acquiescence . . . add up to a
muckheap only violence will shift. Sure, we've known
all along our old ways had to go. Some time. The
reckoning come. Some time. The whirlwind. In
someone's time. The whirlwind is here. In our time —
"All that is gone, Aunt Annie," I said, "all we
depended on for our identity has gone, ourselves
have helped to pull it down." Not all the commissions,
corporations, facelifts in the world can make that
stand again. Our only hope: did the seed of anything

good come out? What — new people we have it in us
to become. "We, is it, now?" she says, "*we*, is it? An'
you safe in Englan' all this time." We went into the
room at the back where — what is left of Lily Martin
lives. Aunt Annie had tried to prepare me. "You not
show your shock now." I clapped eyes on — that
trunk of her, no legs, no arms; the head bald as an
egg, half the features blown away. The breath was
dashed out of me, I had no breath left to try to —
hide my horror. And Lily saw. Three hours out of the
twenty-four she'll sleep now; the other twenty-one
she cries. Cousin Sammy came, was, and is, to marry
her. He stood beneath the picture of the Duke of
Edinburgh and the Queen, in his anorak, cap, dark
glasses; with his stick. "It's well for you," he said,
"across the water. We here have to fight. To save the
land we love." I wanted to say, "There are other ways
to fight." I wanted to say, "This way of ours, what
shall you do to this 'land you love'?" I wanted to say,
"Do I not love this land as well as you?" I've only
to think of the Nine Glens, Lough Fea on Slieve G . . .

> The mountain's name itself he suddenly
> represses.

Sentiment. Think of Bogside, Burntollet, the rotten
wrongness there has been, the wrongness I in my own
acquiescence have been a part of. . . . I love that
land; her I carry. . . . But. . . . Violence will never pay,
we are told. But it does; and in our hearts we know it
does. I have been part of a muck that only violence
can shift. Yet I said to Sam, "Soon or late, this
violence must end. Sooner or later, the bloodshed has
to stop: can't the lesson be drawn from it now?"
I didn't put what I said so bravely, nor so well. I was
frightened. I had to — choose my words. "I just
think," I said, "I just think we have to try to find
some new way, up, out of this, Sammy," I tried to
say, "we have been a great people. Twice in history
our Protestant existence here has turned a tide of
tyranny back: once, against the Catholic monarchies

of Europe; more recently, denying Hitler the freedom
of the ocean — moments not to be underestimated
nor forgotten. Now we are on the anvil a third time.
Can we rise to the occasion this third time, then?
Turn a third tyranny back? The tyranny of our own —

Now it hits COLIN and the clarity of it frees him.

— *inheritance*? Our inheritance *is* glorious: but all
that has to be behind us now. Shed. I just — I just
think we just have to — try to see, what new selves
we can rise up out of this, and become. Oh, Sammy,
if we can do that, oh, then we are a brave tribe."

Perhaps with a hint of Sammy's up-yours
gesture.

"Phoenix yerself." Uncle Tommy's coffin lay in the
front parlour of the house for friends and neighbours
to come filing in and see. "Lord bless us, but he
makes a lovely corpse." Only Tommy's coffin was
closed. Tommy's was closed. One of the neighbour
women even said, "Your Tommy was a large mahn.
His coffin is so small." In the morning, the men all
came to carry him to his grave. I went to put my
shoulder to the coffin to do my share of the bearing.
The men pushed me aside. And Sam said . . .

Quiet, reasonable.

"You'll carry no Ulsterman's coffin to no grave.
Stay here wi' the weemen." The drum beat. Up the
street, to the Orange Hall then to the grave, went
with that coffin all my — belonging. . . . The women
did not speak to me. I felt so severed.

With no self-pity, but an absolute, new clear-
seeing.

I know it is the strongest feeling in the world, to be
alone. And I did feel strong. Yet, the land, from

whose earth I belong, the clan, from whose loins
I come, had turned me out; to my own loins no
child of tomorrow shall come: and I felt so —

At last.

— severed.

There is a long silence.

*He takes out, lights and begins to smoke a
cigarette — the only time anyone smokes in the
play. He peers out the side window of the van
into the dark. For him, though a sorrow, it is
also a setting free.*

So. There's another — "self" for the rubbish heap
with all the rest. My self as "tribal son." Yet: if
we do not change, tomorrow has no place for us.

Blackout.

*We hear someone practising wide-spaced piano
arpeggi, in slow five-finger groups, stepwise
haltingly ascending and descending in C major,
C minor, A flat major, D flat, etc. The chairs
on the set are struck. The lights come up — a
cold light — on a scene with a wheelbarrow and
newdug potatoes. ANNE, in a rough coat, is
seated on the foot of the rostrum sorting
potatoes — those cut or speared in digging, into
a box or basket, for immediate use; the good,
gently, into a bulging half-hundredweight paper
sack; the blighted, on a spread local newspaper,
for discarding.*

ANNE:
Bloody piano. "Exercise to stretch the webs between
the fingers." Why won't he *accept* his hands are too
small? In winter his skin hardens, the webs split and
bleed. I begin to wonder, "Does he only try at what

he knows he can't achieve?" Some sort of escape,
that. Lord grant me learn my proper parish. . . .

The piano music fades.

*A blighted potato breaks between ANNE's
finger and thumb.*

Irishman, and these he grows.

She puts the potato onto the newspaper.

Still. . . . Blight. Good years and bad. Luck. . . .
Husbandry. . . . I could gorge between my legs now
the milk of a thousand men and it all perish, safe.
Stop; stop. Burn these.

An advertisement in the paper catches her eye.

"What is it makes the Arnolds so full of beans?"

Wryly, resuming her work.

What *is* it, makes the Arnolds so full of beans?

*She becomes conscious of a sound the audience
does not hear — electric sawing in the distance.*

Elms being felled. . . . All the parks, fields, farms of
the county, elms being felled. Bark stripped off and
burnt, roots ripped up and burnt. Along the roads
their tall crowns wither, grow bald, their doomed
stems marked with a white painted cross. And the
farmers burn the stubble all over, day and night —
when by law they should not — to burn the wheat-
rust out. And because it's cheaper. Singe the
orchards, burn the hedgerows with their buds and
berries down, because its cheaper. Pillage the earth,
and before it's rested, radge it with a winter crop.
Squeeze the earth dry, she'll last just about as long
as we shall; bugger our sons.

Elsewhere, she hears another sound the audience
does not hear.

Jeff Walton, altering his pigs he's bought. They grub
their own testicles up from the ground where they've
fallen, and eat them. I just remember my dream.
I was teaching the children. Suddenly I said, "Oh
children, all you children, go under, all go under,
quickly, quickly." Outside it was bright blue day.
Such blue. Suddenly I saw in the sky huge vessels
shaped like the upturned abdomens of wasps, striped
yellow and red, yellow and green, upcurling and
vanishing into the blue. I knew what they were. The
air was clammy with a fine invisible mist, in the
sunshine all the people shopping had begun to vomit
and spit. I ran to the chemist's for a sink to puke
in, but his door was padlocked. In all the house
windows, notices: Clean Water Five pee. I came
home. I said, "Colin, I did what I could, I brought
home what I could." But in my basket there was
nothing. I cried at that. I cried such tears, the wild
upwelling that we weep in dreams. He was trying
to make love to me. His penis was arid and red hot.
I was pretending. Suddenly he screamed and leapt
away from me, bent over. "Oh, what's the matter,
my love?" I said, "tell me the matter." He said —
when the seed came out of him, it was scalding spit,
it tore out of his knob like the E string of a violin —
and I saw: it had ripped up and back along his shaft
like a cheesewire. I touched him: I wanted to make
him better. I touched him, his flesh turned hard,
then scaly like a fish. I could see he was dying. He
was — dying — Then he was dead. I came out across
the marsh. The sky was red like blood. The land was
black. The cabbages had been blasted from their
stalks, the stalks stood gnarled and knotted in rows,
unnaturally gleaming. I was weak. I could see my
body was turning scaly as his had done. I dragged
myself to where I could lean against a thorntree. I
lay there. A child came. No child that I could call
a child. A child of ice, moving without seeming to

move, crossing the black flat of the marsh beneath the red sky. He-she-it, featureless, white, its head in a dome like a child from space. I was so frightened, so weak I could not lift myself at all; I felt I was going out, like water down a drain: into extinction. . . .

She thinks, but she does not say, "But no. . . ."
In a new tone, as if a resurrection were coming.

I woke. A voice overlapped from the dream: the child's and mine: the same. "Take *off* your dead" . . .

COLIN enters quietly, wearing an anorak and cords again. He has an opened letter in his hand.

COLIN: *speaking tersely*
From the County.

His face and voice show nothing.

ANNE snatches the letter, glancing at his face, and reads it. COLIN leans his arms upon the rostrumside, reading the newspaper on the ground without taking any of it in, covertly glancing at her. She is looking up, forward, out, the letter in her hand on her lap. COLIN waits until it is time for him to speak. His words are not cold, but inly stricken of all expression.

That's it. Another "us" to shed: mummy and daddy.

He looks down at the newspaper once again. His eye catches something. He speaks with the tiniest chuckle.

"Day-old boy found in lavatory pan in Worcester." The world is like this.

ANNE says nothing. COLIN does not look up. In a there-it-is tone, he speaks . . .

Laughter of children in our house, not for us. Whatever *is*.

> *Yes. Whatever is. This road must now be abandoned also. ANNE sees it; inly she has known it all along. It is pitiful, but they are released. Their hopes for parenthood lie in ashes, but on some other road must lie whatever is for them. After a moment, she turns herself, without standing, toward COLIN, and now he must learn to look at her, frank in his inadequacies, his reality, just as he is, all male personae shed.*

> *A beginning.*

Colours in the Dark — James Reaney
The Ecstasy of Rita Joe — George Ryga
Captives of the Faceless Drummer — George Ryga
Crabdance — Beverley Simons
Listen to the Wind — James Reaney
Ashes for Easter & Other Monodramas — David Watmough
Esker Mike & His Wife, Agiluk — Herschel Hardin
Sunrise on Sarah — George Ryga
Walsh — Sharon Pollock
The Factory Lab Anthology — Connie Brissenden, ed.
The Trial of Jean-Baptiste M. — Robert Gurik
Battering Ram — David Freeman
Hosanna — Michel Tremblay
Les Belles Soeurs — Michel Tremblay
API 2967 — Robert Gurik
You're Gonna Be Alright Jamie Boy — David Freeman
Bethune — Rod Langley
Preparing — Beverley Simons
Forever Yours Marie-Lou — Michel Tremblay
En Pièces Détachées — Michel Tremblay
Lulu Street — Ann Henry
Three Plays by Eric Nicol — Eric Nicol
Fifteen Miles of Broken Glass — Tom Hendry
Bonjour, là, Bonjour — Michel Tremblay
Jacob's Wake — Michael Cook
On the Job — David Fennario
Sqrieux-de-Dieu — Betty Lambert
Some Angry Summer Songs — John Herbert
The Execution — Marie-Claire Blais
Tiln & Other Plays — Michael Cook
The Great Wave of Civilization — Herschel Hardin
La Duchesse de Langeais & Other Plays — Michel Tremblay
Have — Julius Hay
Cruel Tears — Ken Mitchell and Humphrey & the Dumptrucks
Ploughmen of the Glacier — George Ryga
Nothing to Lose — David Fennario
Les Canadiens — Rick Salutin
Seven Hours to Sundown — George Ryga
Can You See Me Yet? — Timothy Findley
Two Plays — George Woodcock
Ashes — David Rudkin
Spratt — Joe Wiesenfeld
Walls — Christian Bruyere
Boiler Room Suite — Rex Deverell
In a Lifetime — Roland Lepage
After Abraham — Ron Chudley
Sainte-Marie Among the Hurons — James W. Nichol

The Lionel Touch — George Hulme
Balconville — David Fennario

TALONBOOKS — THEATRE FOR THE YOUNG

Raft Baby — Dennis Foon
The Windigo — Dennis Foon
Heracles — Dennis Foon
A Chain of Words — Irene Watts
Apple Butter — James Reaney
Geography Match — James Reaney
Names and Nicknames — James Reaney
Ignoramus — James Reaney
A Teacher's Guide to Theatre for Young People — Jane Baker, ed.
A Mirror of Our Dreams — Joyce Doolittle and Zina Barnieh